Teaching for Understanding
Across the Primary Curriculum

D1611477

Multilingual Matters

The Care and Education of Young Bilinguals: An Introduction to Professionals
Colin Baker
The Care and Education of a Deaf Child: A Book for Parents
Pamela Knight and Ruth Swanwick
Computers and Talk in the Primary Classroom
Rupert Wegerif and Peter Scrimshaw (eds.)
Dyslexia: A Parents' and Teachers' Guide
Trevor Payne and Elizabeth Turner
Encyclopedia of Bilingual Education and Bilingualism
Colin Baker and Sylvia Prys Jones
The Guided Construction of Knowledge
Neil Mercer
Language and Literacies
Teresa O'Brien (ed.)
Language Policy Across the Curriculum
David Corson
Language, Minority Education and Gender
David Corson
Learning about Punctuation
Nigel Hall and Anne Robinson (eds)
Making Multicultural Education Work
Stephen May
A Parents' and Teachers' Guide to Bilingualism
Colin Baker
Race and Ethnicity in Multiethnic Schools
James Ryan
Second Language Students in Mainstream Classrooms
Coreen Sears
Studies in Immersion Education
Elaine M. Day and Stan M. Shapson
Teacher Education for LSP
Ron Howard and Gillian Brown (eds)
Teaching and Assessing Intercultural Communicative Competence
Michael Byram
Understanding Deaf Culture: In Search of Deafhood
Paddy Ladd

Please contact us for the latest book information:
Multilingual Matters, Frankfurt Lodge, Clevedon Hall,
Victoria Road, Clevedon, BS21 7HH,England
http://www.multilingual-matters.com

Teaching for Understanding Across the Primary Curriculum

Edited by
Lynn Newton

MULTILINGUAL MATTERS LTD
Clevedon • Buffalo • Toronto • Sydney

Library of Congress Cataloging in Publication Data
A catalog record for this book is available from the Library of Congress.

British Library Cataloguing in Publication Data
A catalogue entry for this book is available from the British Library.

ISBN 1-85359-596-9 (pbk)

Multilingual Matters Ltd
UK: Frankfurt Lodge, Clevedon Hall, Victoria Road, Clevedon BS21 7HH.
USA: UTP, 2250 Military Road, Tonawanda, NY 14150, USA.
Canada: UTP, 5201 Dufferin Street, North York, Ontario M3H 5T8, Canada.
Australia: Footprint Books, PO Box 418, Church Point, NSW 2103, Australia.

Printed and bound in Great Britain by Short Run Press Ltd.

Contents

Editorial:
Teaching for Understanding Across the Primary Curriculum

Understanding is a valued goal in education and yet, because of its polymorphic nature, it is both difficult to define and to describe. It can mean different things to different people in different contexts. Nevertheless, the various guises of the National Curriculum for England and Wales have emphasised skills, knowledge *and* understanding in the different curricular areas to be covered in the primary school. This special edition of *Evaluation and Research in Education (ERiE)* explores what is meant by understanding generally and how teaching for understanding can be achieved by primary teachers in different areas of the National Curriculum.

In the first paper in this collection, Douglas Newton draws upon his expertise in this area and provides an overview of what is meant by understanding generally. He discusses why understanding is important and the varied forms it can take. He concludes by exploring how the construction of understanding can be supported.

The core areas of the National Curriculum are considered in the next five papers. In the second, Sue Beverton draws on her expertise in language and linguistics to explore the place of teaching for understanding in delivering the National Curriculum Order for English in the primary school. Understanding in the area of mathematics is discussed by Andrew Davis in the third paper. Andrew's varied interests in assessment, philosophy and early years mathematics are all reflected in his discussion of what counts as understanding in primary school mathematics. Teaching for understanding in primary science is discussed by me in the fourth paper. The nature of understanding in science is considered and strategies which teachers can use to support children in developing scientific understandings are discussed. In addition, in the fifth paper, Tony Blake takes a particular aspect of science – geology – to discuss his research into supporting understanding in this area of experience. The final aspect of the core curriculum, information and communications technology (ICT), is discussed by Steve Higgins in the sixth paper and Steve's interest in mathematics is drawn upon to exemplify how ICT can be used by teachers.

That there is more to the curriculum than the core areas of English, mathematics, science and ICT is acknowledged in the remaining papers in the collection. In particular, many primary teachers recognise the importance of the creative and expressive arts and the humanities in the primary school and yet the current focus on standards in literacy and numeracy and externally imposed assessment procedures have tended to marginalise these areas of experience. The humanities are considered in papers seven and eight, where John Halocha discusses teaching for understanding in geography and I explore understanding in primary school history. In the ninth paper, Peter Millward and Anthony Parton join forces to discuss the essential nature of creative and expressive experiences in the primary school and the place of developing understandings within these experiences.

That we need to acknowledge the importance of an early start in thinking about teaching for understanding is emphasised by Eve English in the tenth and final paper in the collection. Drawing upon her expertise as a past infant school head teacher and early years specialist, Eve reviews the Foundation Curriculum document from the perspective of learning with understanding in the very early years. She considers the nature of learning at this stage generally and the pursuit of understanding in particular.

The collection of articles is intended to provide a starting point for primary practitioners to think about teaching for understanding. It should be of interest to those currently in training, newly qualified teachers and teachers of many years experience. We hope it provides a springboard for further reading and research as well as ideas for action in the classroom.

Lynn D. Newton
University of Durham School of Education

Helping Children to Understand

Douglas P. Newton
University of Newcastle upon Tyne, Department of Education, St. Thomas'
Street, Newcastle upon Tyne NE1 7RU, UK

The nature of understanding and why it is of value is discussed. While understanding cannot be transmitted, a teacher can press for it and support it. Ways of doing this are described in broad terms. Some tendencies and obstacles to teaching for understanding are outlined.

Understanding

Understanding is both a mental process and a mental product. Bartlett (1932) described the process of understanding as a mental attempt to connect something that is given with something other than itself. More recently, Nickerson (1985) has described it as 'the weaving of bits of knowledge into a coherent whole'. The ability to notice patterns, connections, correlations and relationships is probably innate (Caine & Caine, 1994). It can order the world and make it more predictable – a distinct advantage when it comes to survival – but this does not mean that we always use the ability successfully.

Perkins (1986) has pointed out that we understand for a purpose in school and the product of understanding is a knowledge of the structure of the topic, the structure's purpose, and why it serves that purpose. The product is different in different subjects and there can be various kinds of understanding in any one subject. For example, in mathematics, there can be an understanding of patterns, concepts, notations, procedures, equivalences and relationships amongst numbers. In English, there is the understanding of narrative, the relationships between characters, and the structure of the plot. In science, there can be understandings of concepts, procedures, states and events. History, too, has its understanding of events, but this is not like that of science because the nature of causation is different (Evans, 1997). Understanding as inferred relationships and mental structure, however, may not be everything. Reid (1986) has complained of an assumed dualism in understanding in which cognition counts and feelings do not. Music, for instance, has been described as a metaphorical description of a situation but, as Serafine (1986) has pointed out, 'it is not clear what people are knowing or mentally doing when they engage in the business of music'. Nevertheless, she defined music as the product of a search for relationships between tonal-rhythmic events and the identification of melodic, harmonic and rhythmic patterns; but any mental structures could be very different to those derived from words. Similarly, fine art has been described as 'a form of cognitive expression which communicates ideas, feelings and emotions'(Seefeldt, 1995). For Thomas (1991), works of art have significance rather than meaning and some prefer 'insight' to 'understanding' (Hirsch, 1967). Taken together, this makes a wide family of mental products we call understanding (Wittgentstein, 1958).

So far, understanding has been discussed as a mental particular; but another way of looking at it is in terms of what it does (Fodor, 1998). Instead of asking about what is represented in the mind, Perkins (1994) has also described understanding as 'the ability to think and act flexibly with what one knows'. This side-steps the question of what enables a mental flexibility and points to an attribute generated by understanding. Hence, a mental configuration which bestows this attribute is understanding. Nevertheless, knowing something of the mental configuration may guide teaching.

All understandings are personal but, in some subjects, certain understandings are favoured. For instance, the understandings taught in science are endorsed by the community of scientists and the teacher is often required to target them. In other subjects, understanding can amount to making connections of a unique, personal significance, as when reading some kinds of poetry. A teacher's role is to foster the construction of understandings and have children reflect upon them. In all contexts, understanding has an emergent quality. Zazkis (1998) writes that, 'to understand something better means to assimilate it in a richer and more abstract schema'. More than that, understanding may expand and change over time as it is extended or re-organised.

Why Understand?

Why concern ourselves with understanding? Repetition is an effective way of committing information to memory. It may be tedious but it can be quicker and easier than achieving an understanding. Why not memorise what we need to know?

Some events, like fastening shoe laces, are essentially the same every time we meet them. Memorising how to deal with them is generally adequate. But each day is never an exact re-run of the previous day. Understanding confers flexibility in thought and action so it can help us respond appropriately to novel events. Consequently, it imparts feelings of competence and confidence. It enables us to think for ourselves, make reasoned choices, evaluate ideas and avoid exploitation (Halford, 1993; Johnson-Laird, 1985; Meijer, 1991). But this is not all. The historian, Henry Adams, said, 'I don't give a damn what happened, what I want to know is why it happened' (Miller, 1996). People like Adams seek an understanding of situations that may have little immediate or practical consequence. The process is a creative one that offers some intrinsic satisfaction. In practice, understanding may satisfy several personal needs at one and the same time. It is a powerful and satisfying way of knowing.

Understanding can also facilitate further learning. For example, Hiebert and Wearne (1996) studied children's learning in mathematics as they moved through grades 1 to 4 (6 to 9 years). In the children's earlier years, teaching was centred on understanding place value, addition and subtraction. The children were not taught algorithms but had to develop their own procedures and explain them to others. Hiebert and Wearne found that this understanding helped the children make sense of later instruction. There was increased retention, greater competence and more rapid progress. This is not to say that those who understood always gave more correct answers in tests: correct answers can often be obtained without understanding. The gains were in the speed of learning new procedures, in answering novel questions and in retaining new material. Given that understanding is a good thing but is in the hands of the learner, can it be fostered?

Pressing for an Understanding

To press for understanding is to require children to deploy their mental resources in a positive attempt to construct a relevant understanding. Consider a mathematics lesson in which the teacher sets a problem for the children to solve. She moves from group to group and monitors progress, helping where she feels it appropriate. She is not satisfied with unsupported descriptions of procedures but persistently asks for explanations, justification, elaboration and reasons (Kazemi, 1998). When the children's mental resources are insufficient for the occasion, a teacher who presses for understanding may attempt to improve those resources and support the child's mental processes.

Teachers with very different ways of working can press for understanding. Garnett and Tobin (1988) describe the lessons of two Australian teachers. One tended to use whole class teaching, identifying prerequisite knowledge and skills, providing logical frameworks and clear explanations and linking new knowledge to old knowledge. The relevance of the work was made explicit and his questions demanded more than recall. The other used a lot of independent work, the learners had a significant amount of responsibility for their own prog- ress and the teacher was more like a facilitator. The students tended to support one another while the teacher ensured that learning was appropriate. Yet, in different ways, both teachers pressed for understanding as both had it as a prime goal and were single-minded about reaching that goal. What is it that makes a press for understanding?

A press for understanding is not tied to a particular teaching strategy. It arises more from the concerns, inclinations and expectations of a teacher and can be present in a variety of ways of working. Applied to children, a press for under- standing is likely to be accompanied by support for the thinking processes that construct understanding and some provision that motivates the children to engage those processes.

Explaining, direct experience and problem solving

Since understandings cannot be transmitted, merely telling children the rela- tionships in some topic seems unlikely to provide much of a press for under- standing. Nevertheless, explaining can work, particularly when attention is given to its form and content. For instance, a conceptual model such as an anal- ogy or an example can highlight what is important and make connections easier to notice (Mayer, 1989). Beck *et al.* (1991) illustrate how explanations can be improved by giving attention to background knowledge, providing information to activate an appropriate context, clarifying connections between events, and avoiding ambiguous or distant references and an unduly high density of concepts. Children, however, might listen to these explanations but not attend to the parts that matter and fail to establish relevant relationships. Explanations only stand a chance if a child engages with them in appropriate ways. Direct experience of what is to be learned, as in some forms of practical activity in science, is often assumed to be good for understanding simply because it is direct but it is similarly constrained. In practice, the outcome depends crucially on chil- dren's prior knowledge. Even when that is adequate, it does not guarantee a worthwhile outcome (Asoko, 1996; Cavalcante *et al.*, 1997). Problem solving is also commonly assumed to be good for understanding. In practice, it may fail because children may choose to work backwards from the goal. This can be effective in solving the problem but may not greatly enhance understanding (Sweller, 1994). Such strategies often lack a press for understanding and support for its processes.

Questioning to press and support understanding

The learning context may neither press nor support understanding so children's thinking may go nowhere or anywhere. There will be times when their mental engagement could benefit from orientation and direction. At the same time, the teacher may need to monitor the child's thinking. Questioning can do both and, in doing so, provide a press for understanding. Some kinds of question are better at this than others (Newton & Newton, 2000). When questions are directed towards relationships, causes and effects, and reasons, they encourage the integration of ideas and related facts into the coherent wholes we call understanding (Newton, 2000; Scrctny & Dean, 1986; Sundbye, 1987). For instance, asking learners for an explanation in their own words is known to enhance understanding, presumably because it obliges them to make the mental connections needed to construct a response (Chi *et al.*, 1994). A more focused example is when asking for a forced prediction. A forced prediction requires a learner to predict subsequent states (Newton, 1994). A simple example would be: In the series of numbers 2, 5, 11, 23; what would be next? A task like this usually requires a fairly detailed mental processing of the relationships in the information (Harlen, 1985; McNay, 1993 and see Newton, L.D., this issue: pp. 143–153, 182–188).

Such questions can focus attention on what matters and increase the likelihood that a relationship will be constructed. These questions are also asked in the expectation that the child will construct an answer. To the extent that the expectation is fulfilled, questions press for understanding, direct it and support it, and give the teacher some insight into the child's thinking which can guide further questioning. Oral interaction of this kind can respond to a child's thinking immediately and re-direct it as needed. This immediacy makes for a persistent press.

Of course, the teacher does not have to ask the questions. *Critical Squares* is a game-like activity that directs thought towards producing an understanding (Tishman & Andrade, 1997). For example, one activity comprises tasks arranged in a Noughts and Crosses grid. In the 'Whyzit' game (the Whyzit being, for example, the topic of *Civilisation*), one task is, 'All players: Brainstorm at least four ways to change the Whyzit *(Civilisation)* to make it better...' The sequence of games is intended to mobilise prior knowledge and direct attention to what matters on the way to an understanding. In the process, it presses for understanding. The games are intended to induce particular kinds of thinking in the learner in an ordered way so they progress from orientation to constructing understandings in a topic. While it takes some of the demand off the teacher, it cannot respond to an individual's particular thinking needs.

Beyond the Press

While we may press and support children's thinking, we would probably prefer that they worked at it themselves. Can we teach them what they need to do to understand? At one level, probably not. As Smith (1992) says, 'No-one has to learn to think' as it is probably an intrinsic property of the structure of the brain. But, while most children have the necessary hardware, not all construct an understanding successfully. It could help, of course, if children recognise those occasions when they do not understand. Very young children may not be aware of their thinking or use self-help strategies intentionally or consciously. Young learners can regulate their learning after about four years of age but they need support to do it (Pressley & Ghatala, 1990). When asked if they understand, children may say yes but that should not be taken at face value (Barnett & Hixon, 1997). By 10 years of age, however, there seems to be a fairly shrewd idea of what constitutes understanding in others. For instance, children are more likely to select someone who says that the lesson 'hangs together' than someone who says it was 'enjoyable' (Newton & Newton, 1998). Given these constraints, a teacher may try to inculcate ways of thinking that will be deployed unconsciously.

While 'the equipment, ability, and general predisposition to think may be innate ... specific ways in which we make sense of the world are learned' (Meyers, 1986). For instance, what counts as causal understanding in science is not the same as in history. Saying that the Spanish Armada sank because the ships were too heavy for their size would not attract praise in history, just as in science the response that the ships were in unknown waters in a storm would not be accepted. What counts has to be learned because understanding is context dependent.

A carefully structured press for understanding could help children acquire potentially productive habits of thought. It may also be possible to teach certain aids to thinking. For example, constructing a graphic organiser – a scaffold in the form of a story map, picture, diagram or chart – can guide thought (Adger *et al.*, 1995; Roth, 1990). At times, the teacher might model thinking towards an understanding by asking and answering questions herself. In modelling the recall of prior knowledge, she might ask, 'What do I already know about ... ?' 'Where have I seen this kind of thing before?' She might continue, 'Now I have to explain why ... so I need to find out about ...' She might end, 'Have I explained why?' In due course, she might become more reticent and expect the children to think towards understandings themselves. A press for understanding also shows children that it is a valued product. The products let them know what counts in a given subject. With older children, knowledge of the attributes of what counts could be made conscious through discussion.

We should not, however, assume that every child is willing to make the mental effort to understand. Motivation is also important. Eccles and Wigfield (Wigfield, 1994) consider that learners' perceptions of the value of the task and their expectation of success are the primary determinants of learning behaviour. To have value, the task must offer something the learner desires, wants, needs, believes to be important or sees as worthwhile. This could be a longer break, a gold star or praise but it could also be the instrinsic interest and perceived relevance that the task offers. Relevance is not something that is necessarily apparent to young children and it may help if it is made explicit. Practical utility is what might come to mind first but care is needed as not all that is considered worthwhile can be justified on such grounds. Learners are also more likely to engage in a task if they feel that they have some control over it (Deci *et al.*, 1991). This may be achieved by allowing some flexibility in what is done and how it is done. The expectation of success can be coloured by prior experience and, in particular, how the learner attributes past success and failure. If the cause of failure is felt to be outside the learner's control, motivation is likely to be low. Goals should be clear, specific and achievable. Modelling what is expected may help and effort should be rewarded as that is in the learner's control. Tests of learning need to give some reason for maintaining a positive expectation (Newton, 2000). Pintrich and De Groot (1990) add emotion to value and expectation. The risk of shame or humiliation can result in task avoidance (Ingleton, 1995). The difficulty with anxieties of this sort is that they are complex, but learning needs to be managed to minimise the risk of such feelings. In effect, the intention is to develop children's mental resources so that they are able to engage successfully and willingly in the construction of understanding (Bailin, 1998).

Beyond 'Makes-sense'

Typically, when people construct an understanding, they reason to a 'makes-sense' state and persist with that (Perkins *et al.*, 1991). Children may use their resources to reach such a state but, of course, it may be neither the best that they could achieve nor an understanding that is acceptable. But a press for understanding may take it further. When the makes-sense state is unacceptable, it may be necessary to help the child construct an alternative framework. If the makes-sense state is generally satisfactory, a teacher may feel it could be richer, deeper, wider and, where appropriate, capable of application. Pressing the child to relate what they know to other knowledge, establish new relationships, use them and justify that use could help to achieve that end.

Lemke (1990) has pointed out that learners can be good at giving us the answers we want to hear. They build 'understandings' that may not connect with their existing knowledge. These may serve to answer questions, complete exercises and take part in lessons, but are isolated structures, held without conviction and sometimes at odds with existing knowledge. The teacher needs to take questioning further and develop it into purposeful 'conversations' that heal the gaps between these proto-understandings and existing knowledge. These conversations may be initiated and maintained by gentle questioning, but responses are not curtailed or re-directed. Instead, the child is encouraged to expose the fuller structure of his or her thought by elaborating upon responses and talking around it. The teacher's role is to help the child relate understandings to existing structures and examine the points at which understandings break down.

Some Obstacles

Although understanding is often a stated goal, it can be a secondary concern. There are many possible reasons. Where there is a factory model of education that 'adds value' and an emphasis on the transmission of knowledge, and where schools are condemned publicly for apparently not adding value, a teacher's attention is likely to be directed towards obtaining high test scores at any cost. Where schemes of work are overcrowded or tests ask mainly for the recall of information, a teacher is likely to play down understanding and aim for memorisation. Understanding takes time and giving that time to memorisation can have short-term benefits. The long-term loss, of course, is to the child. Further, understanding is something the child must do; the processes can be supported but an understanding cannot be transmitted from teacher to child. If constructing an understanding is difficult, supporting it seems to demand even more of the teacher. There can be a silent compact of understanding avoidance between some teachers and some children (Gardner & Boixmansilla, 1994). Even when there are good intentions, teachers are usually more expert in some subjects than in others. As a result, they may not press equally for understanding in all areas (Newton, 1999; Newton & Newton, 1997, 1998, 1999, 2000).

An Exacting Task

This serves to illustrate the inherent complexity of the task of supporting a child's understanding. Furthermore, 'we neglect the uniqueness of the [thinker] at our peril' (Tweney, 1991) so this complexity is multiplied many times in the classroom. Pressing for understanding is often taxing and teachers would have to be superhuman if they were not tempted by transmitting facts and descriptions. This is not to imply that these are unimportant: there can be no understanding without 'facts'. When, however, they become a society's or a teacher's main concern, the school's gift to the child is diminished.

Correspondence

Any correspondence should be directed to Professor Douglas Newton, Department of Education, University of Newcastle, St Thomas' Street, Newcastle Upon Tyne NE1 7RU, UK (d.p.newton@ncl.ac.uk).

References

Adger, C.T., Kalynapur, M., Blount Peterson, D. and Bridger, T.L. (1995) *Engaging Students: Thinking, Talking, Cooperating.* London: Sage.

Asoko, H. (1996) Developing scientific concepts in the primary classroom: Teaching about electric circuits. In G. Welford, J. Osborne, and P. Scott (eds) *Research in Science Education in Europe* (pp. 36–49) London: Falmer.

Bailin, S. (1998) Education, knowledge and critical thinking. In D. Carr (ed.) *Education, Knowledge and Truth* (pp. 204–20). London: Routledge.

Bartlett, F.C. (1932) *Remembering: A Study in Experimental and Social Psychology.* Cambridge: Cambridge University Press.

Barnett, J.E. and Hixon, J.E. (1997) The effects of grade level and subject on student test score predictions. *Journal of Educational Research* 90, 170–4.

Beck, I.L., McKeown, M.G., Sinatra, G.M. and Loxterman, J.A. (1991) Revising social studies text from a text processing perspective. *Reading Research Quarterly* 26, 251–76.

Caine, R. and Caine, G. (1994) *Making Connections: Teaching and the Human Brain.* Alexandria: Association for Supervision and Curriculum Development.

Cavalcante, P.S., Newton, D.P. and Newton, L.D. (1997) The effect of various kinds of lesson on conceptual understanding in science. *Research in Science and Technological Education* 15, 185–93.

Chi, M.T.H., Leeuw, N de., Chiu, M-H. and LaVancher, C. (1994) Eliciting self-explanations improves understanding. *Cognitive Science* 18, 439–78.

Deci, E.L., Vallerand, R.J., Pelletier, L.G. and Ryan, R.M. (1991) Motivation and education: The self-determination perspective. *Educational Psychologist* 26, 325–346.

Evans, R.J. (1997) *In Defence of History.* London: Granta.

Fodor, J.A. (1998) *Concepts.* Oxford: Clarendon.

Gardner, H. and Boixmansilla, V. (1994) Teaching for understanding in the discipines and beyond. *Teachers College Record* 96, 198–218.

Garnett, P.J. and Tobin, K. (1988) Teaching for understanding. *Journal of Research in Science Teaching* 26, 1–14.

Halford, G.S. (1993) *Children's Understanding.* Hillsdale: Lawrence Erlbaum.

Harlen, W. (1985) *Teaching and Learning Primary Science.* London: Harper Row.

Hiebert, J. and Wearne, D. (1996) Instruction, understanding and skill in multidigit addition and subtraction. *Cognition and Instruction* 14, 251–83.

Hirsch, E.D. (1967) *Validity in Interpretation.* New Haven: Yale University.

Ingleton, C. (1995) Gender and learning. *Higher Education* 30, 323–35.

Johnson-Laird, P.N. (1985) Mental models. In A.M. Aitkenhead and J.S. Slack (eds) *Issues in Cognitive Modelling.* Hove: Lawrence Erlbaum.

Kazemi, E. (1998) Discourse that promotes conceptual understanding. *Teaching Children Mathematics* 4, 410–4.

Lemke, J.L. (1990) *Talking Science.* New Jersey: Ablex.

Mayer, R.E. (1989) Systematic thinking fostered by illustrations in scientific text. *Journal of Educational Psychology* 81, 240–6.

McNay, M. (1993) Children's skills in making predictions and their understanding of what predicting means: A developmental study. *Journal of Research in Science Teaching* 30, 561–77.

Meyers, C. (1986) *Teaching Students to Think Critically.* San Fransisco: Jossey-Bass.

Meijer, W.A.J. (1991) Factual knowledge and understanding. *Religious Education* 86, 74–82.

Miller, A.I. (1996) *Insight of Genius.* New York: Springer-Verlag

Newton, D.P. and Newton, L.D. (1997) Teachers' conceptions of understanding historical and scientific events. *British Journal of Educational Psychology* 62, 184–92.

Newton, D.P. and Newton, L.D. (1998) Enculturation and understanding. *Teaching in Higher Education* 3, 339–63.

Newton, D.P. and Newton, L.D. (1999) Knowing what counts as understanding in different disciplines. *Educational Studies* 25, 43–58.

Newton, D.P. and Newton, L.D. (2000) Do teachers support causal understanding through their discourse when teaching primary science? *British Educational Research Journal,* in press.

Newton, D.P. (1994) Supporting the comprehension of tabulated data. *British Educational Research Journal* 20, 455–63.

Newton, D.P. (2000) *Teaching for Understanding.* London: Falmer.

Newton, L.D. (1999) Teaching for understanding in primary science. Paper presented at the 4th Summer Conference on Primary Science Teacher Education, University of Durham, July 1999.

Nickerson, R.S. (1985) Understanding understanding. *American Journal of Education* 93, 201–39.

Perkins, D.N. (1986) *Knowledge Design.* Hillsdale: Erlbaum.

Perkins, D.N. (1994) *The Intelligent Eye.* Santa Monica: The Getty Center for Education in the Arts.

Perkins, D.N., Faraday, M. and Bushey, B. (1991) Everyday reasoning and the roots of intelligence. In J.F. Voss, D.N. Perkins and J.W. Segal (eds) *Informal Reasoning in Education.* Hillsdale: Lawrence Erlbaum.

Pintrich, P.R. and De Groot, E.V. (1990) Motivational and self-regulated learning components of classroom academic performance. *Journal of Educational Psychology* 82, 33–40.

Pressley, M. and Ghatala, E.S. (1990) Self-regulated learning: Monitoring learning from text. *Educational Psychologist* 25, 19–34.

Reid, L.A. (1986) *Ways of Understanding and Education.* London: Heinemann.

Roth, W.M. (1990) Map your way to a better lab. *The Science Teacher* 57, 30–4.

Seefeldt, C. (1995) Art – a serious work. *Young Children* 50, 39–42.

Serafine, M.L. (1988) *Music as Cognition.* New York: Columbia University.

Seretny, M.L. and Dean, R.S. (1986) Interspersed post-passage questions and reading comprehension achievement. *Journal of Educational Psychology* 78, 228–9

Sweller, J. (1994) Cognitive load theory, learning difficulty, and instructional design. *Cognition and Instruction* 4, 295–312.

Smith, F. (1992) *To Think.* London: Routledge.

Sundbye, N. (1987) Text explicitness and inferential questioning. *Reading Research Quarterly* 22, 82–97.

Thomas, R.S.D. (1991) Meanings in ordinary language and in mathematics. *Philosophia Mathematica* 13, 37–50.

Tishman, S. and Andrade, A. (1997) *Critical Squares: Games of Critical Thinking and Understanding.* Englewood: Teacher Ideas Press.

Tweney, R.D. (1991) Informal reasoning in science. In J.F. Voss, D.N. Perkins and J.W. Segal (eds) *Informal Reasoning in Education* (pp. 3–16). Hillsdale: Lawrence Erlbaum.

Wigfield, A. (1994) The role of children's achievement values in the self-regulation of their learning outcomes. In D.H. Schunk and B.J. Zimmerman (eds) *Self-regulation of Learning and Performance* (pp. 101–126). Hillsdale: Lawrence Erlbaum.

Wittgenstein, L. (1958) *Philosophical Investigations.* Oxford: Basil Blackwell.

Zazkis, R. (1998) Odds and ends of odds and evens. *Educational Studies in Mathematics* 36, 73–89.

Whatever Happened to Primary English Knowledge and Understanding?

Sue Beverton
University of Durham, School of Education, Leazes Road, Durham DH1 1TA, UK

A rather particular set of problems has characterised the question of primary English subject knowledge and understanding. True, the definition of the English subject understanding that primary pupils should acquire has long been problematic. However, what primary *teachers* should know and understand about the English language in order to teach it has been the prior worry. Consequently, what, if any, *knowledge about language* primary pupils should understand in order to learn the English they are taught has also been at the centre of long debates. These debates have added to deep uncertainties about how primary English as a subject should be defined and what its purpose is. The present paper begins by summarising chronologically the main issues in these uncertainties. The paper then looks at what English subject knowledge teachers have been considered over time as needing to know. The paper concludes that compared with other curricular subjects primary English is a special case: it is a nebulous subject that has long been prey to socio-political forces. Consequently teachers need to redefine their professional understanding of the subject.

The History of the Definition and Purpose of Primary English

Prior to the beginning of the 20th century, understandings of the nature and purpose of English as a primary school subject were influenced by legacies from more classical, traditional concepts of the school curriculum. While 19th century public secondary school curricula were dominated by instruction in Greek and Latin, the majority of the nation's secondary-aged pupils received teaching in the English language and literature because, the view was, of the civilising influence and 'moral wealth' that such instruction would produce (Knight, 1996: 34). Also, as the century drew to a close, the subject-based organisation of the secondary curriculum was heavily influenced by the universities. They set the examinations by which entry to universities was determined, thus English Literature figured prominently in secondary curricula. However, English as a primary curriculum subject was not examined, explored, questioned or considered. The content of the primary curriculum was defined by its role, which was to instruct pupils in the '3 Rs', and prepare them for their secondary education.

A turning point came soon after the First World War, with the publication of the Newbolt Report (HMSO, 1921). The Newbolt Committee had been charged with inquiring into the position occupied by English in the educational system of England, and to advise how its study may best be promoted in schools of all types. While the Committee's report did see English language teaching as a means of saving the nation's children from poor speech habits, it also exposed the inappropriateness of teaching grammar using Latin grammar as a template. Most significantly, it distinguished between the use of prescriptive and descriptive grammars of English as textbooks. This can now be seen as an early stage in what has become a lengthy controversy over which approach to English grammar should be adopted in primary schools. Newbolt compromised in seeing the study of language as best being kept simple and basic, but also important. The report spoke of the fundamental role of English (literature and language) in forming cultural knowledge and in realising experience. It emphasised the common cultural heritage embodied in English as a school subject. Thus it provided a role for English and reasons for all teachers to teach English that went far beyond compensatory models of the previous century, reasons that included a way of finding '... *a bridge across the chasms which now divide us*' (HMSO, 1921).

During the 1950s and 1960s the status of English as a school subject became more established, in particular at secondary level with the branching of English into two examinable aspects, Language and Literature, although debate continued over their content and purpose. Within primary education, while well established as a subject in its own right, the nature of primary English came into dispute. Essentially, the debate was between members or factions within the teaching profession and was not entered into by politicians, academics or others. Broadly different approaches emerged during this period concerning the questions of what primary English was and what purpose it served. On the one hand, the view of English having a culturally enriching, self-developing role had many adherents. For others, English was more of a means to an end, a more communications-orientated discipline. As one might expect, different pedagogic practices subsequently stemmed from such views: child-centred pedagogy, promoted by such influential bodies as the Plowden Committee (reporting in 1967), resonated with the ideas that the role of English was to provide a means of absorbing values, releasing self-expression and responding to literary experience. One example where this approach became especially prominent was the teaching of reading, where discovery methods enabled children's understanding of language features, forms and functions. Courses in language awareness and the celebration of multilingualism flourished. Others, however, saw all this as a threat to view that culture was a 'given' (Dixon, 1975) and to the previously secure place of grammar teaching (Knight, 1996).

During the early 1970s there was concern at policy-making levels that primary English needed to be reviewed and sharpened. Control over the debate moved away from members of the profession. Indeed, we may see what followed as a significant step by government to intervene in the hitherto education professionals' domain of setting the primary English curriculum. Attention began to focus upon the English language as a means of communication requiring the development of certain skills. In 1972 a Committee of Inquiry, chaired by Sir Alan Bullock, was established. It considered in relation to schools:

> ... all aspects of teaching the use of English, including reading, writing and speech; how present practice might be improved ... and the role that initial and in-service training might play ... and to what extent arrangements for monitoring the general level of attainment in these skills can be introduced or improved. (DES, 1975: xxxi)

The resulting Bullock Report, *A Language for Life* (DES, 1975), stressed the role of English as the medium through which teaching and learning is largely conducted. It promoted the notion of 'language across the curriculum', meaning that all subjects carried a responsibility towards developing pupils' language. The report had a subsection on 'Language Study' (under 'Written Language') in which the development of pupils' understanding of how language functions is advised through teaching about language in context. *A Language for Life* did not support de-contextualised grammar teaching, that is, grammar teaching for its own sake, and eschewed a prescriptive approach to defining the grammar of English.

By *A Language for Life* taking the view that grammar was best seen as a description of real language, the controversy between prescriptive and descriptive grammatical schools of thought was temporarily laid to rest. Most importantly, however, from this report two linked themes emerged that would each provide grounds for dispute for many years: they are *Knowledge About Language* (KAL) and Standard English.

Advocates of the importance of KAL as part of the English curriculum appeal to a deep-rooted sense of language as experience. In essence, they appeal for the teaching of the grammar of the English language *as it is used*. For them, the term grammar is a broad church, carrying no preconceptions as to one particular correct version. KAL allows for the exploration of how language changes under different conditions, how people speak differently from each other and from how they may write. It aims to develop language awareness (LA), in which pupils and teachers develop a sensitivity to KAL. Understanding and using grammatical terms are seen as useful in analysing and describing different forms and functions of language (Crystal, 1995).

Proponents of KAL take issue over stipulations that Standard English 'should' be taught on the grounds of its being 'correct'. They would take the view that there is not one single variety of English, spoken and written, that should assume an exclusive position as *the* form of English language in the curriculum. Indeed, to reach a situation in which English in primary schools was based on Standard English would be to risk rejecting the validity of other varieties. Standard English itself has no local base, although it is seen by linguists as *a* variety of English, standing alongside but not above, other dialects of English. Standard English is seen not a matter of pronunciation, it may be spoken in a wide variety of accents. In England there exists a prestige accent, Received Pronunciation (RP) in which Standard English is often spoken. Standard English is mainly distinguishable by its grammar and orthography (spelling and punctuation) and is recognised by adult members of the community as having prestige value.

During the 1980s, HMI published a series of discussion documents on curricular aims and content. *English from 5 to 16: Curriculum Matters* (DES, 1984) drew heavily upon the *A Language for Life* in its philosophy upon the centrality for learning of achieving competence in the use of English. It stated that:

> All teachers, whatever their other responsibilities and whatever age groups they teach, have a contribution to make to this process ... (of aiding their pupils to achieve competence in the many and varied uses of English)'. (my brackets – DES, 1984: 1)

English from 5 to 16 established four aims for the teaching of English, of which the fourth, admitted as likely to be the most controversial, was to teach pupils *about* language (that is, KAL). This was necessary as a means of increasing pupils' ability to use and respond to language. *English from 5 to 16* acknowledged the confusion that had existed for many years over whether grammar should be explicitly taught. Rejecting formal drills and exercises as the way to teach grammar, HMI stated its preference for teachers and pupils giving attention to language, examining its structure and how it works. The governing factor on the question of what and how much grammatical terminology pupils should be taught was '... how much they could assimilate with understanding and apply to purposes they see to be meaningful and interesting' (DES, 1984: 14)

In 1988 Professor Brian Cox was appointed to lead a working party to devise programmes of study and attainment targets for English within the National Curriculum. Cox had been a member of the Kingman Committee (see below) that had reported that year on what training teachers should have about English. Cox's working party's first report, which contained sections on Standard English and grammar and linguistic terminology, was amended at the insistence of Kenneth Baker (the then Secretary of State for Education). Baker's insistence was upon the primacy of a Latinate style of English grammar to be unequivocally stated . This made it difficult for Cox and his working party to get across their Kingman-inspired view that while grammatical knowledge and understanding were important, they should be developed through descriptive, generative grammars, with appreciation of the diversity of grammars that exists for English. In the published version of the first report (DES, 1988b), however, the concept of 'grammar' was given a more prominent role and expressed in firmer language than in the working party's first report. A section on Standard English, however, was retained. This was later explained by Cox himself as possibly because of government confusion over the difference between Standard English and Received Pronunciation (Cox, 1991: 25).

The struggle between government and those charged with advising it over finding acceptable definitions of English and its purpose in the curriculum probably reached its height at the time of the two Cox reports (DES, 1988b; 1989a). Since then the decline of an independent voice that spoke for informed, apolitical views on the nature and role of English, has been marked. An early casualty was the curtailment of the 'Language in the National Curriculum (LINC) Project (1989–1992)'. This was a government-funded initiative set up, as recommended in the Kingman Report, to provide training for serving teachers in Knowledge About Language. Its official materials, intended for publication, were banned in 1991. Government silence accompanied the prohibition. Since then, revisions to the National Curriculum have contained sections on 'Standard English and Language Study' (DfE, 1995) and 'Standard English' and 'Language Variation' (DfEE/QCA, 1999) although their prescriptions have remained at the level of general blandishments.

English Literature in the primary curriculum has also been exposed to some, but not so much, public controversy. Perhaps the debates over the place and nature of English Literature in the secondary curriculum were sufficient. The close association in primary schools between quality reading material, whether literature or non-fiction, and successful English teaching was not seriously challenged. Yet for many years government agencies have made uninspired references to 'literature'. Banal requirements, such as the one that pupils should read '... poems or stories with familiar settings and those based on imaginary or traditional worlds ...'. (Key Stage 1, English AT1, DfE, 1995: 6), are virtually unchanged in the curriculum for 2000 (see DfEE/QCA, 1999: 46).

One potentially powerful legacy of those years is the model of the five roles for English that Cox presented (DES, 1989a: 21). These were, in brief, that English in the curriculum provides:

- a means of 'personal growth';
- has a 'cross-curricular' role as a medium of instruction;
- meets an 'adult needs' role as a communication tool;
- carries a 'cultural heritage' function;
- enables 'cultural analysis' through a critical understanding of the world.

What English Subject Knowledge Should Primary Teachers Possess?

It would seem reasonable to suppose that the teachers who have to teach a primary curriculum for English do actually need to possess some relevant knowledge in order to teach it. What and how much is a problem. There does not appear to be a substantial body of evidence to answer this. Instead, there is more by way of worthy advice. From the previous section it is not surprising to find that the question of specifying what knowledge of English primary teachers should possess was highly politicised for most of the 20th century, from the Newbolt Report onwards. The next landmark came in 1988, when the Kingman Committee was established by the then Secretary of State for Education, Kenneth Baker. The job of this committee was to recommend what training teachers should be given in order to understand how English works and to identify what, in general terms, pupils also need to know about how the language works (KAL again). The timing of this was critical: the Kingman Committee can be seen as pivotal, occurring between the appearance of the HMI papers including *English 5 to 16* and the formation of the working group, chaired by Brian Cox, to specify the English National Curriculum and Attainment Targets.

From the start the Kingman Committee sparked controversy. Its membership was widely seen as an insult to the teaching fraternity (Rosen, 1988: 2). Teachers were not represented and the views held by its members were assumed to be strongly pro-government (that is, in favour of Latin-based teaching of grammar, and supporting the view of the correctness of Standard English, for example). When it reported, however, teachers and politicians were surprised. The Kingman Report (DES 1988a) contained a thoughtful, sensitive model of the English language that was novel to many, being descriptive rather than prescriptive, and influenced by a functional view of language. In answering its brief of specifying what training teachers should receive and what pupils needed to know it took full account of the preceding debates over KAL and LA (see above). It observed:

> We believe that within English as a subject, pupils need to have their attention drawn to what they are doing and why they are doing it because this is helpful to the development of their language ability. It is important, however, to state that helping pupils to notice what they are doing is a subtle process which requires the teacher to intervene constructively and at an appropriate time. (DES, 1988a: 13)

Unsurprisingly, the report did not fully please government. This was widely seen at the time as mainly because it did not advocate a return to the traditional style prescription and teaching of a Latinate grammar. At the time of its appearance, many major new developments such as the ERA and the introduction of the National Curriculum rather overshadowed Kingman's message, and its advice lay largely unheeded by government. The hand of governmental alterations to the Cox Report, mentioned in earlier, illustrates the weak impact of the Kingman Report.

There is some sign that during the 1990s the overt tension between government and profession over specifying what knowledge of English primary teachers should possess lessened. Questions over KAL and Standard English were less often and less openly discussed. But beneath the apparent decline of those arguments a deeper struggle continued over who should identify the language knowledge that primary teachers should possess – professional educators (teachers, academics, researchers) or those ultimately employing teachers, the government. As the 1990s drew to a close, definitive government directives appeared which signalled the end of those battles. The National Literacy Strategy Training Pack (DfEE, 1998b) is one example of such directives. These in-service training materials contain videos, teaching resource sheets and information for teachers. Widely used as preparation for the National Literacy Strategy, these materials, and more recent ones such as Additional Literacy Support (ALS) Materials (DfEE, 2000a), may have a major impact upon teachers' approach to language teaching. Embodying a government stance on what is 'best practice' and appearing firm and full of conviction, they offer primary teachers a 'security blanket', removing the necessity for them to explore and develop a well-formed philosophy of their own of the role and nature of English in the Curriculum. They render the role and nature of what knowledge of English teachers need to possess as unproblematic. This flies in the face of the concerns of previous decades.

Where Are We Now?

There are other difficulties with these government-issued directives. The Framework for Teaching (both the original (DfEE, 1998b) and the 2000 2nd edition) and the National Curriculum for Primary Initial Teacher Training, English (DfEE, 1998a) do not contain consistent messages about language information. DfEE Circular 4/98, *Teaching: High Status, High Standards*, rather blandly and blithely presents the view that what is English subject knowledge is unproblematic. Yet the National Curriculum has moved towards seeing this differently. For example, as early as Key Stage 1 the English Programme of Study specifies that pupils should be '… introduced to some of the main features of spoken standard English and be taught to use them'. (DfEE 2000b: 45) as well as advising teachers, confusingly, that:

> The paragraphs on standard English, language variation, language structure and language structure and variation in speaking and listening, reading and writing provide a coherent basis for language study.

Perhaps this discord, between primary English being portrayed as an unproblematic subject that is amenable to positivist definition and direct transmission on the one hand and being acknowledged as variable, changing and flexible on the other, is not very important. Teachers may teach largely in accordance with their own beliefs about the subject-matter they are attempting to convey. But is English too important to be abandoned in the centre of such a tug-of-war? While the debates have waxed and waned, and waxed and waned again, the actual content of primary English *as taught* has outgrown all definitions. Rather like a pre-adolescent child who has put on almost overnight a growing spurt that surprises even its parents, what is now commercially available to teachers as advice and materials for teaching language has grown enormously in recent years in range, quantity and quality. One thing this suggests is that we are about to lose the subject identity of 'English' in the primary school. Another is that teachers are steering a rudderless course through a sea of ideas and understandings about language and English. A professionally-run review of where English is as a primary subject is urgently required. That way teachers will redefine their English subject knowledge and understanding for themselves.

Correspondence

Any correspondence should be directed to Dr Sue L. Beverton, University of Durham, School of Education, Leazes Road, Durham DH1 1TA, UK (s.l.beverton@durham.ac.uk).

References

Cox, B. (1991) *Cox on Cox: An English Curriculum for the 1990's*. London: Hodder and Stoughton.

Crystal, D. (1995) *The Cambridge Encyclopedia of The English Language*. Cambridge: Cambridge University Press.

Department for Education (1995) *English in the National Curriculum*. London: HMSO.

Department for Education and Employment (1998a) *Teaching; High Status, High Standards Requirements for Courses of Initial Teacher Training (Circular 4/98)*. London: DfEE.

Department for Education and Employment (1998b) *The National Literacy Strategy Framework for Teaching*. London: DfEE.

Department for Education and Employment/Qualifications and Curriculum Authority (1999) *The National Curriculum Handbook for Primary Teachers in England*. London: HMSO/QCA.

Department for Education and Employment (2000a) *Additional Literacy Support Materials*. London: HMSO.

Department for Education and Employment (2000b) *The National Literacy Strategy Framework for Teaching* (2nd edn). London: HMSO.

Department of Education and Science (1975) *A Language For Life* (The Bullock Report). London: HMSO.

Department of Education and Science (1984) *English From 5 to 16 Curriculum Matters 1 An HMI Series*. London: HMSO.

Department of Education and Science (1988a) *Report of the Committee of Inquiry into the Teaching of English Language* (The Kingman Report). London: HMSO.

Department of Education and Science (1988b) *English for Ages 5 to 11* (The Cox Report). London: HMSO.

Department of Education and Science (1989a) *English for Ages 5 to 11* (The Second Cox Report). London: HMSO.

Department of Education and Science and the Welsh Office (1989b) *English in the National Curriculum*. London: HMSO.

Dixon, J. (1975) *Growth Through English – Set in the Perspective of the Seventies*. Oxford: NATE and Oxford University Press.

HMSO (1921) *The Teaching of English in England (The Newbolt Report).* London: HMSO.
Knight, R. (1996) *Valuing English.* London: David Fulton Publishers.
Rosen, H. (1988) *Struck by a Particular Gap.* In A. West and M. Jones (eds) *Learning Me Your Language: Perspectives on the Teaching of English.* Cheltenham: Stanley Thornes.

Teaching for Understanding in Primary Mathematics

Andrew Davis
University of Durham, School of Education, Leazes Road, Durham DH1 1TA, UK

Mathematics consists of a complex interconnected set of concepts and rules. These 'exist' within the practices of adult communities. Individual learners have to assimilate these concepts by making appropriate connections with what they already know and by means of appropriate interactions with expert communities. Mathematical understanding that is worth having can be used and applied in the real world in a flexible fashion. In the light of this account, and of the high stakes testing regime currently in force in the United Kingdom, some aspects of the National Numeracy Strategy do not seem well designed to support the development of mathematical understanding. The paper advocates a return to some classroom mathematics in which pupils have a degree of control.

Mathematics and Mathematical Understanding

Mathematics consists of a complex interconnected set of concepts. No single item can be thoroughly grasped without reference to others. A child begins to understand '5' when she appreciates at least some of an indefinite number of linked mathematical points, including the fact that it is 1 more than 4, 1 less than 6 and that it is the sum of 3 and 2. In fact, the meaning and significance of any particular number cannot really be comprehended without at least some idea of the number system as a whole. Addition cannot be grasped without realising its relationship with subtraction and the way in which it operates within the set of natural numbers, the integers and ultimately the set of real numbers. The very *identity* of any particular mathematical concept is bound up with its relationships to others. Mathematical ideas are not discrete objects which, so to speak may be added one by one to the mind or removed in similar style. A better comparison to illustrate the character of their existence might be with the positions of pieces on a chessboard. The 'position' of my rook has no meaning on its own. It derives its identity from its relationship with the rest of the board.

So far this account makes no reference to the physical universe. If no more were said, mathematics might be appropriately characterised as 'the subject in which we never know what we are talking about, nor whether what we are saying is true'(Russell, 1917). However, mathematics enables us to communicate in an exact and analytical fashion about aspects of the world. It can be used and applied. With numbers we can make precise claims about an indefinite variety of empirical phenomena. Measurements and comparisons may be given accurate expression and we can estimate the probability of events using a numerical scale.

Pure mathematics has been viewed by some as an uninterpreted system, having reference to nothing beyond itself. This is a very abstract notion of the subject, perhaps not easily grasped except by its advanced practitioners. In its everyday and scientific use it forms part of the language in which we identify phenomena and attribute properties to them.

The connectedness of this discipline then extends beyond the links between mathematical ideas as such. There are relationships to empirical concepts. For instance, we cannot exhaust the 'meaning' of subtraction merely by specifying the sets of numbers to which this operation may be applied, its relationship to addition, and so on. Something must also be said about the way in which it may be modelled in the 'real world'. It can be illustrated by means of the physical removal of objects from a group and by the physical comparison of one group of objects with another. These are just two of the possible models. More would be needed for an adequate characterisation of subtraction.

Consider a second example of relating mathematics to the world. Euclidean geometry can be seen as an axiomatised system about 'lines' (which have no thickness and indeed no physical existence), possessing properties such as 'straightness' (defined internally within the system). However its status as a geometry rather than as a peculiar self-contained logical system depends on the possibility of a physical interpretation in the space of our universe.

There are two distinct sets of connections at issue here. First, there are internal links between mathematical concepts. Second there are 'external' links between mathematical concepts and ideas about the real world. The former set of connections may be characterised comprehensively, at least with respect to the current accepted developments in the subject. The properties of subtraction in that sense may be listed, and the best person to do that for us would be the professional mathematician. Applying mathematics to empirical phenomena in contrast covers an open-ended and potentially infinite set of connections. There are any number of potential applications of subtraction to real situations, even if these applications fall into a modest number of broad categories.

Evidently mathematical understanding must be a matter of degree, if this 'connected' vision of the subject is correct. A young child cannot suddenly, in a 'single spasm of seamless cognition' (Fodor & Lepore, 1992) come to understand all the aspects of, say multiplication. She must start somewhere. She will initially encounter some primitive mathematical building blocks as unconnected cognitive elements. As such they will have little or no meaning for her. However, by the time she is beginning to master language, and long before she experiences formal schooling, she has already begun to assimilate mathematical ideas in the form of interconnected networks.

There is no such thing as a 'full' or 'complete' understanding, for at least two reasons. First, the subject of mathematics itself is not 'finished'; it is always in a state of development (and sometimes revision). Second, learners can always make more comprehensive connections within their own minds, or revise the connections already made.

Mathematical understanding worth having involves the ability to use and apply mathematics in a flexible fashion in the variety of contexts encountered in adult life. A necessary condition for the usability and applicability of mathematics is that it is appropriately connected in the mind of the learner. For too long our education system has turned out 'rule-bound' adults possessing half-remembered mathematical rules without having any idea of how and why they work. At best such people can offer some correct answers in mathematical tests in familiar formats. They certainly cannot use their mathematics. In short, they have developed little understanding of it.

Psychologists and educators broadly agree that most young children acquire mathematical concepts by interacting with the world and learning to talk about it in specific ways in the company of adult or more expert users of mathematical language and concepts (e.g. Lave & Wenger, 1991; Vygotski, 1978). It is possible to build on to this story an account of the existence of mathematics itself as embodied in the rules and practices of communities. Ernest (1991) and others refer to this account as *social constructivism*. Children developing mathematical understanding are learning to talk and think mathematically about the world in the company of more advanced users of the rules. They are also learning to operate within the rules themselves, and about the connections between them, even when there is little or no reference to the world. To sum up, they acquire understanding of both pure and applied mathematics by means of appropriate social interactions.

Mathematics is certainly not the only subject whose central concepts are interconnected. Many scientific concepts are bound together in a similar fashion. For instance, within Newtonian mechanics, the meaning of 'force' is intimately linked to its relationships with 'mass' and 'acceleration'. Indeed ideas in any subject are interconnected, though in less regimented fashion than those within mathematics and science.

Nevertheless it is especially important to emphasise this feature within mathematics, since it has implications for the way in which understanding of the subject can develop. Mathematics has sometimes been seen as the paradigm case of a subject that may be learned in a logical and linear sequence. For instance, it has been held that children should learn to count before tackling long multiplication. They should master simple functions before being offered differential calculus.

However this picture is too crude. When children move from earlier to later material, the mastery of the later material rebounds upon and enriches the earlier content. Children will encounter fractions after operations with whole numbers. Yet their work with whole numbers was not in a sense 'finished' or 'complete' at the time and the understanding of fractions transforms their prior ideas about number. Robert Dearden (1968) suggested that when we are thinking about these issues we often commit what he called the *'fallacy of perfected steps.'* The fallacy is to suppose that 'one thing must be perfectly, and not just partially, understood before one can move on to the logically next thing'. It is also a familiar point that even if we can reach agreement about what it means for A to be logically prior to B, it does not follow that we should learn A before B, let alone learn A 'completely'.

The National Numeracy Strategy and Mathematical Understanding

Government policy is decidedly ambivalent in its approach to the development of children's mathematical understanding. *The National Numeracy Strategy* (DfEE, 1999) emphasises a version of numeracy that on first reading appears to incorporate the kind of connectedness referred to above. Teachers are encouraged to make 'links between different topics in mathematics and between mathematics and other subjects' (DfEE, 1999: 5). They should include 'some non-routine problems that require (pupils) to think for themselves'. Pupils are supposed to 'have a sense of the size of a number and where it fits into the number system', to be able to draw 'on a range of calculation strategies', to be able to explain 'their methods and reasoning' and to be able to 'judge whether their answers are reasonable and have strategies for checking them where necessary' (DfEE, 1999: 4).

On the other hand the Strategy suggests that the children in each class should 'work together through the year's programme described in the Framework, so that all children participate when a new unit of work starts and can take part in the plenary' (DfEE, 1999: 2). There is no explicit recommendation that teaching should proceed regardless of whether children seem to be learning. Yet anecdotal evidence suggests that many schools follow their medium-term plans while paying little attention to children's day-to-day progress. They might justify such decisions by pointing out that the Yearly Teaching Programmes laid down by the Strategy involve 'revisiting' the same concepts a term later, or half a term later.

This theme of 'keeping the children together' could be interpreted as a move away from supporting individual understanding construction and towards teaching for a group mastery of superficial mathematical performances. Are teachers really supposed to ignore at least in the short term the failure of some pupils to grasp the concepts taught in any particular lesson? If so, the policy raises questions about the type of understanding sought by the Numeracy Strategy. Have they forgotten that each individual *must* build understanding on whatever idiosyncratic set of concepts and relationships they bring to the mathematics lesson?

Proponents of the Strategy could enthusiastically deny this. They could claim that through the differentiated group work in the middle part of the numeracy lesson, by means of appropriate questioning and the explanation by pupils of their reasoning and methods in whole class situations, support for personal understanding construction is still in place.

Such claims would be more plausible if made independently of the current UK system of employing test performance as part of school and teacher accountability. It may be argued that the high stakes testing regime militates against the development of understanding, and instead rewards teachers who maximise test performance regardless of whether a richer understanding is being built up. For this argument to succeed a number of assumptions must hold good:

- Tests cannot probe a 'rich' connected understanding in such a way that they combine a satisfactory level of reliability and validity. Instead they 'measure' thin proceduralised knowledge because that is the only kind of knowledge which they can deal with reliably. High levels of reliability are essential in high stakes assessment.
- Teaching to maximise test performance is not teaching which will promote the development of richer understanding, at least in the short term.

The first assumption is not one that can be investigated empirically. If it is true, it is necessarily true. In Davis (1998) I have argued that it is necessarily true. Space does not permit that argument to be rehearsed here. The second assumption is partly a matter of principle and partly susceptible of empirical investigation. If teachers follow OfSTED advice and inform children of the learning outcomes they intend at the beginning of the lesson, they ought to be honest about their intentions. In the current system these will be to maximise behaviours resembling the sought after test performances. In theory they could intend that pupils perform well on tests as a direct result of developing a rich understanding of the relevant mathematics. However such an intention may not seem very sensible given the short time scale typically available to the primary teacher. Teachers would be forgiven for thinking that it is less risky and more effective in the short term to teach directly for the test performances required. That is, they employ strategies, which are most likely to elicit from pupils the required performances regardless of whether the pupils are making appropriate connections between the relevant concepts and skills in order to produce the performances in question.

Developing Children's Mathematical Understanding

The current teaching strategies advocated by the government are heavily weighted in favour of teacher control. Teachers determine the mathematical level of their teaching and of the tasks they set for their pupils. They announce the objective to be achieved at the beginning of the lesson, and are encouraged to measure their own success according to whether the pupils acquire the learning outcomes specified in their opening announcement. What differentiation is permitted is very firmly a 'differentiation by task' in which the teacher is supposed to know the attainment level of her children and to set the work accordingly (but only in up to three attainment levels spread across up to four groups). Teachers are encouraged to 'keep the class together'; crude records are kept of whether children have attained 'key objectives' at the end of particular blocks of teaching. Now the devisors of the National Numeracy Strategy must ultimately be concerned with the development of individual pupils' mathematical understanding. After all, what else could be the point of 'reforming' primary mathematics teaching? Yet overt references to such individual development within the documentation provided are hard to find.

If understanding growth depends at least in part on opportunities to build new knowledge in appropriate social contexts on the basis of what is already known then perhaps current strategies may be less than ideal. Given the complexity and idiosyncrasies of personal understanding it may be argued that pupils should exercise a degree of control over aspects of their learning. I will briefly elaborate on just two elements of this argument.

First, pupils know at least as much about their own understanding of mathematics as their teachers. Hence choices about for instance the level at which they might work will be at least as well informed as their teachers' choices would have been. Significant levels of pupil decision-making may be encouraged within *mathematical investigations* in which pupils choose methods and sometimes even what questions to address. 'Investigations' were given official approval by the Cockcroft Report in 1982 (Cockcroft, 1982) and were quite popular a decade or so ago.

Second, each child's understanding base will differ to a degree from others. 'New' learning will vary in its impact from one pupil to another. One pupil may well need material in a different order from another, or more repetition, or to return to earlier ideas in a different way from another, and so on. We need not exaggerate the extent to which individual learning paths differ from each other to plead for a limit to teacher control over the detail of individual learning.

The National Numeracy Strategy, with its 'key objectives' and high degree of structure is admirable in many ways and teachers who believe themselves less than adequate in the subject feel suitably supported by the materials and the training. Yet there is a very strong emphasis on top-down planning, on the idea that teachers know best about precisely what and how children should learn, and about the techniques to deliver this. A deeper understanding of the truth in constructivist accounts of the development of understanding would lead to placing more emphasis on pupil control than is recommended by current policy.

We will look at one important illustration of this. The Strategy encourages children to talk about and to develop their own personal and mental calculation strategies. It hints that certain types of written recording may help to support the development of competence in mental calculation. Children might be encouraged to use 'empty number lines' in various ways for this purpose.

It seems an excellent idea for pupils to be made aware of this possibility of a visual support for their mental method. However, they certainly should not be *trained* to use a particular procedure rigidly. Below is a typical example from the National Numeracy Strategy (1999) to help children use a mental strategy to add 86 and 57.

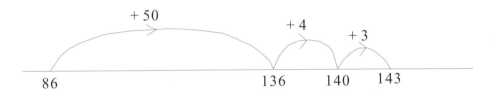

This type of recording features in some official training materials offered by the Strategy. It is to be hoped that it will not become part of a new set of 'rules without reason' imparted to generations of pupils whose bewilderment will be equal to that of earlier generations when taught the equal addition subtraction algorithm. If teachers are not very careful they may find themselves *teaching* children to record using the empty number line regardless of whether that form of representation is helpful for every individual child. Many children will find it useful, but for some it might even prove counterproductive. Methods may vary quite legitimately from one individual to another. Moreover, the best calculation method to use depends in part on the numbers concerned.

Conclusion

The connected character of mathematical concepts and rules and the social constructivist perspective on the nature and status of mathematics point to the idiosyncratic and individual nature of understanding development. This in turn suggests that pupils should retain a measure of control over their own learning. Despite the undoubted strengths of current policies in the United Kingdom designed to 'raise standards' there are real tensions between these policies and ensuring that pupils develop a rich understanding of mathematics which they can use and apply in flexible fashion as adults.

Correspondence

Any correspondence should be directed to Dr Andrew Davis, University of Durham, School of Education, Leazes Road, Durham DH1 1TA, UK (A.J.Davis@durham.ac.uk).

References

Cockcroft, W. (chair) (1982) *Mathematics Counts.* London: HMSO.
Davis, A. (1998) *The Limits of Educational Assessment.* Oxford: Blackwell.
Dearden, R. (1968) *The Philosophy of Primary Education.* London: Routledge and Kegan Paul.
DfEE (1999) *The National Numeracy Strategy.* Cambridge: Cambridge University Press.
Ernest, P. (1991) *The Philosophy of Mathematics Education.* Basingstoke: Falmer Press.
Fodor, J. and Lepore, E. (1992) *Holism: A Shopper's Guide.* Oxford: Blackwell.
Lave, J. and Wenger, E. (1991) *Situated Learning: Legitimate Peripheral Participation.* New York: Cambridge University Press.
Russell, B. (1917) *Mysticism and Logic.* London: Unwin Books .
Vygotsky, L.S. (1978) *Mind in Society: The Development of Higher Psychological Processes.* (M. Cole, V. John-Steiner, S. Scribner and E. Souberman, eds). Cambridge, MA: Harvard University Press.

Teaching for Understanding in Primary Science

Lynn D. Newton
University of Durham, School of Education, Leazes Road, Durham DH1 1TA, UK

The requirements of the National Curriculum Order for Science (DfEE, 1999) are such that children must be provided with opportunities to acquire not only the skills that underpin the process of Scientific Enquiry (Sc1) but also the knowledge and understandings fundamental to Life Processes and Living Things (Sc2), Materials and their Properties (Sc3) and Physical Processes (Sc4). This is a tall order for most primary teachers, particularly those for whom science is not a specialism. In this paper, what counts as understanding in science is discussed. The problems facing primary teachers in pressing for understanding are considered. Some ways of encouraging and enabling them to support the construction of understanding are also suggested. In particular, the importance of focused questioning is discussed.

Introduction

Understanding is a worthwhile and valued goal in education because of its enabling properties. It can satisfy curiosity, promote feelings of confidence and competence and facilitate further learning (Newton, 2000). So what counts as understanding in science? According to Nickerson (1985: 202), understanding in science is:

> ... the connecting of facts, the relating of newly acquired information to what is already known, the weaving of bits of knowledge into an integrated and cohesive whole ...

It is about getting a handle on things, getting the message, making mental connections between facts, concepts, ideas and procedures. In science, this often involves a search for patterns in order to find unifying principles and explain cause-and-effect relationships. For Piaget (1978), only those mental structures that answer the question 'Why?' deserved to be called understanding. These figure in science a lot of the time.

There are several kinds of understanding in science, including conceptual, procedural, situational and causal (Newton, 2000). *Conceptual understanding* is what we expect when we say a child understands ideas such as energy or respiration. Both of these are scientific concepts and each involves other, more fundamental concepts. These need to be related to what already has meaning for the child, that is to the child's prior knowledge and understanding. In turn, they would be knitted together to form a coherent whole.

An understanding of ways of doing things, particularly in connection with practical work, is what we usually describe as *procedural understanding*. Not only must the children comprehend the sequence of activities or procedures; they must also know the reasons that explain and justify what they do. As with conceptual understanding, it should be underpinned by and linked with well-founded knowledge.

Situational (or *descriptive*) *understanding* involves an exploration of a situation in which the child must grasp what it amounts to and describe it. For example, through their various experiences, the children notice and describe how a mirror produces an inverted image or the stages in the life cycle of a moth. This kind of understanding could also involve both conceptual and procedural understanding.

An event that involves some change in a situation and a grasp of the cause-and-effect relationship is *causal understanding*. While we want children to know that one thing leads to another, we also want them to understand why. This means that we want them to connect an initial situation with a final situation by making causal connections. Such understanding must usually be well-founded on prior knowledge and experience so that it makes sense to them. Causal understanding is particularly important in understanding the world. For example, the children's past and present experiences of light from a torch and light and mirrors lead to them explain why light can be reflected from a mirror onto a wall in a predictable way. This enables patterns to be noticed, predictions to be made and explanations to be generated.

As a goal in science teaching, the National Curriculum Order requires an understanding of life processes, materials and physical processes. The attainment targets set out the 'knowledge, skills and understanding that pupils of different abilities and maturities are expected to have at the end of each key stage' (DfEE/QCA, 1999: 74)

In all cases it is a shift from *knowing and describing* at Key Stage 1 (Level 1 and 2) to *describing and explaining* at Key Stage 2 (Levels 3 to 5). Pupils are expected to demonstrate an increasing knowledge *and* understanding of phenomena, events and situations in science as they progress through the levels from Key Stage 1 to Key Stage 2. For example, for *life processes and living things*, at Level 3 pupils should:

> use their knowledge and understanding of basic life processes when they describe differences between living and non-living things. They provide simple explanations for changes in living things. (DfEE/QCA, 1999: 76)

Trainee primary teachers in England and Wales are also to be made aware of the importance of ensuring that their pupils progress from describing phenomena and events to explaining them. They must be able to make understanding an explicit target in the science activities they plan and be able to support the children's thinking to increase the likelihood that they will understand (DfEE, 1998). Pressing for understanding is to interact with children in a way that requires them to make a mental effort to construct understanding (see the earlier paper by D.P. Newton). To what extent do primary teachers press for understanding in science teaching?

The Current Position

In one research study, 50 Key Stage 2 primary science lessons were observed in Year 3 (7–8 year-olds) to Year 6 (10–11 year-olds) classrooms in schools in the North-East of England (Newton & Newton, 1999). The content of the lessons was classified according to the nature of the discourse and the activities provided. There was evidence that there was generally little press for understanding. Factual recall and description tended to be emphasised. Further, the press for understanding with the younger children (the 7–9 year-olds) tended to be less than with the older children (9–11 year olds). There was also evidence that the emphasis placed on understanding by non-specialists tended to be less than that of science subject specialists.

This research supplements the evidence from the USA, Canada and Australia, which indicates that understanding may not be a priority in the classroom. For example, the research of Bruer (1994); Gardner and Boix-Mansilla (1994); Sierpinska (1994); Wildy and Wallace (1992) all indicate that what often counts is a facility in reproducing information. An additional problem is that the children themselves may fail to see understanding in science as an important goal, perhaps suggesting that the teacher's emphasis lies elsewhere (Newton & Newton, 1998). What might account for such neglect?

First, primary teachers may recognise the importance of understanding and value it yet still not give it a high priority in the science classroom since parents, governors, inspectors and politicians are only concerned with performance indicators, league tables of results and SAT (standard assessment test) scores. A press for information recall and the reproduction of facts may give them most of what is needed. Second, pressing for and supporting understanding in the primary science lesson can be more demanding than rehearsing facts and recalling information. Teachers have to engage with a pupil's response at a deeper level than is needed for recognising and acknowledge a correct answer to a factual recall question. Third, strategies used to teach for and support understanding can take time. If the amount of science material to be covered is large and time is short, then understanding may suffer. Finally, the above all assume that teachers see understanding as a significant goal in science. This may not always be the case. In the UK, primary teachers are usually expected to teach all subjects although their own subject expertise may be in only one or two areas. With at least 10 National Curriculum subjects to be covered, science may not have figured highly in such teachers' own education. While some can hold appropriate conceptions of the nature of science and what counts as understanding in science, many do not (Newton & Newton, 1998). Even those with a degree in a science subject have been found to hold narrow and even inappropriate conceptions of the nature of science and what counts as understanding.

In such circumstances, it is not surprising that many primary teachers direct their efforts towards supporting the quantity and reproduction of science knowledge rather than to promoting quality in learning with understanding (Newton & Newton, 1999). Children who are not pressed for understanding may, in turn, develop a view of science where factual recall is what is seen as important. This could hinder later learning. What can be done to promote teaching for understanding in primary science?

Ways Forward – Encouraging and Supporting Understanding in Science

What underpins a primary teacher's classroom behaviour is complex. They hold many and varied beliefs and conceptions about science, the nature of science, teaching and learning, children's capabilities and a teacher's own breadth and depth of subject knowledge. All probably shape classroom behaviour. In addition, the kind of understanding a teacher wants to encourage will shape the kind of activity chosen to support the process in the science lesson. There are a number of types of activity to promote understanding:

- explanations;
- models;
- analogies;
- discussions;
- practical work;
- games;
- focused questions; and,
- bridging.

Understanding through explanations

When explaining how something works, why it is the way it is, or the reason for something happening as it does, concrete structures should be provided that the children can use to think with. For example, when attempting to make the point that there are such things as life cycles, specific exemplars, such as the frog or butterfly, should be chosen and set that out in a form which makes it more likely that the relationships or patterns will be noticed. Since it is likely the teacher wants to establish a generalisation about life cycles, other examples should be added to this, but not at the outset. The aim is to establish the idea *then* extend it. Finally, to make it clear that not all animals follow this pattern, a structure for a mammal or bird could be provided, where metamorphosis does not take place in this way. In short, the concept is introduced with an example, developed and widened and then its limits pointed out (Newton, 2000).

Understanding through models

Providing concrete structures is known to be very supportive and often memorable. Models can have the same effect. For example, some young children think that water comes from walls, quite literally. The tap is simply a device which is plugged into the wall and the water drains out through the tap. The sight of a damp wall can reinforce this idea. Of course, ripping out the pipes behind the tap and tracing them back to the water supply is not a practical option. Instead, a model may have to be used to illustrate the real state of affairs. If this can be followed by a visit to the cloakroom to point out the pipes and the water tank, all the better. The model and real world will then be connected (Newton, 2000).

Understanding through analogies

Analogies also provide conceptual structures that can support understanding. They behave something like 'models in the mind' (mental models) and give the children something to think with that is easier to handle than the real thing. For example, the child's world stretches away from them to the horizon and has hills and valleys which are significant bumps and hollows but we tell them that the Earth is a sphere, and a fairly smooth one at that. Having the children truly grasp (as opposed to agree to) the insignificance of the bumps and hollows in the scale of things is not always easy. Using the analogy of an orange can help. An orange has bumps and hollows which can be seen even without a magnifying glass but the orange still looks relatively smooth from a distance. If a hollow represents the valley where our town is, a really strong magnifying glass would be needed to see the town, let alone the people in it. The immensity of the Earth in comparison to the heights and depths of mountains and valleys is introduced with the use of a concrete, visible object with which the children are familiar (Newton, 2000).

Other examples of this kind are in comparing the insect's hollow proboscis with a straw, the skull with a crash-helmet, and bones with card tubes. In the same way, a teacher might use the way a ball bounces off a wall as an analogy for the way light reflects from a mirror. Knowing the way the ball behaves allows the children to predict what will happen in the case of light. It used to be assumed that young children could not think analogically but that has been shown to be unfounded. What is important is that what the teacher chooses to use for the analogy has to be well-known to the children and the children need to know what they are supposed to do with it. Even in the ball-bouncing analogy for the reflection of light, although we can assume that children have played with a ball, they may not have noticed the effect the teacher is interested in or, more likely, it may not be in their consciousness. They need to be reminded of the real thing, what happens and what part of it is relevant before using the analogy (Newton & Newton, 1995).

Understanding through discussion

Discussion is, by definition, a two-way affair. An element of discussion is often present in explanation when children seek to clarify something or a teacher checks that they are following what is being said. Here, while the teacher may be steering the course of the discussion and have particular ends in mind, children are intended to make a very significant contribution. For instance, an outcome might be an explanation, a justification or a design for an investigation generated by the children with guidance. However, for a discussion to be fruitful, children need to know how to engage in it and they need to be suitably seated so that discussion is facilitated. Some teachers prefer a circle but other seating may work well. Whatever physical arrangements are used, it is important to establish it as a routine. Finally, the children need some basic rules about speaking, listening, responding, turn-taking and respectful behaviour to one another (Newton, 2001).

Suppose the intention is to open up and explore the topic of *Clothes*, leading to the properties of the fabrics used for garments with different functions with young children. The teacher might begin with a picture of people in different kinds of weather and ask the children what time of year each is and what the differences are they can see. The next key question could be: Why do people wear different things at different times of the year? Do they wear different things? What is best to wear on a cold morning? What makes it best? Some fabric samples might be passed around to examine. Which is their favourite? Why? Would it be good to wear on a warm day? Why? Magnifying glasses might be passed out at this point for a closer examination of the fabrics. What does waterproof mean? Why do they think this one is waterproof? How could we test it like a scientist to see if it is really waterproof? The children's collective responses and their evaluation of each leads to a design for a simple experiment which compares the fabrics for this property. The children now do the investigation and could be gathered together again for a concluding discussion about what they found. Their new knowledge might now be extended by a discussion of what things they might use the waterproof material for other than for clothing, asking for justifications of their choices.

During teacher-led discussions of this kind, there may also be the opportunity for the teacher to *model* his or her own thinking. This is when they respond to a question or are faced with a problem and think out aloud for the children. For example, a light bulb will not come on in a simple circuit so the teacher begins, 'Let me see, now. Both wires are on the battery and the battery is a new one. I wonder if the bulb is OK. Let's hold it up to the light. Yes it looks OK, there's the filament all in one piece ...' This lets the children see *and* hear the non-random, step-by-step process which underpins the fault finding process. On the next occasion, the teacher may have them do the same thing and talk it through aloud in that way while he or she listens. A different situation is when demonstrating a practical procedure: 'Now the first thing I should do is ... because ... Hmm. It hasn't moved much. I'd better change the ruler for one with millimetres on it, that would suit it better. Next, I must be sure I keep it fair so I'll ...' Notice how the teacher can demonstrate the reasons for the actions and hence show the children that the reasons are important. Similarly, when exploring a causal link, it might be appropriate to say, 'Oh, look! That must be *because* ...' This modelling serves several functions. First, it lets the children know there is a rational basis for things and that this is what matters. Second, it lets them hear thinking processes 'in action' and brings them to awareness so it can be discussed with them. Third, it provides a pattern for them to follow (or, probably more precisely, for them to follow in reporting on their thinking).

Discussion can also take place on a child–child basis. Young children who have practised discussion with their teacher's support may try it on a small group basis. However, the teacher will still need to provide a structure for them to work to, at least to begin with. This could be to break down a discussion into steps and the children are given one step at a time to discuss. There is, however, a danger to be aware of with pupil–pupil discussion in science. Science is not a subject of arbitrary understandings. We aim to develop children's understanding in the direction of the understandings accepted in science as a discipline. While this may develop as hoped in a child–child discussion, it is also possible that misconceptions will be propagated. A vocal and popular child who believes that a fruit floats if it has hollows for its seeds could disseminate that idea widely. This means that group discussions of this nature need to be monitored or, at least, checked in a plenary session when ideas are aired.

All talk with young children should, of course, be considerate. That is, it should use words and linguistic structures children can grasp readily. For instance, use of a chronological sequence when explaining often helps children grasp an event or set of instructions more easily. At the same time, gaps should not be left in an explanation, in the belief that what is left out is obvious. Either telling it all or, better still, asking the children what happens next is more appropriate. While teachers will have to use scientific vocabulary, they should try to begin with simpler terms, then pair them with the scientific terms, and finally use the latter alone. For instance, begin talking about 'push apart', then 'push apart: the proper word is repel', then 'repel, remember that means push apart' and, finally, 'repel; what does that mean?'.

Understanding through practical work

Many primary teachers have a preference for 'hands-on' practical activities in science. While this is a worthwhile strategy, for some teachers it could become an end in itself and even an escape from promoting and supporting understanding. Practical work in science can serve several functions and sometimes more than one at the same time and so teachers must be clear as to what they want the practical work to do. If the aim is to develop conceptual understanding, have the children produce some effect simply to experience it, speculate on its causes, and generally discuss how it relates to other things. For instance, they might try out various kinds of magnet on things around the classroom to learn what a magnet is and can do. It may be possible to include in it some measurement and focus the children's attention on the patterns in the data and the relationships they suggest. The children, for example, dip a magnet in a bowl of paper clips and count the clips on different parts of the magnet to illustrate that the certain parts of the magnet are more significant than others (Newton, 2000).

If, on the other hand, the intention is to develop investigative skills and procedural understanding, an activity might be designed specifically to develop understanding of the control of variables. The teacher might ask, for instance: Which material would be best to use on the floor where everyone seems to slip as they come in? In essence, what is wanted is for the children to test a variety of surfacing materials such as, cork, carpet, vinyl and concrete. The test they are to carry out has to be fair so they need to control the variables. It may be possible to have the children open up the situation through discussion and then plan their investigation. As a result, we would want to see their understanding of variable control improve but, at the same time, it is likely that their understanding of the properties of materials would also benefit. While the follow-up discussion would include a review of fair testing, it should also include a review of this new knowledge to ensure that it is well-integrated with existing knowledge.

Since an investigation seems to offer two gains for the price of one, could the teacher always begin a topic with an investigation? The answer is that it depends on the topic. If it is one where the children already have some reasonably well-founded knowledge, then it is possible to use this to develop ideas for testing. The children will have enough subject background to draw on in their planning. As a result, they may develop both procedural and conceptual understanding. If, on the other hand, the topic is one for which there is not a great deal of background knowledge, its absence appears to hinder progress and little is gained. In this situation, conceptual understanding should have priority and, once there is a foundation, can be developed into investigations (Cavalcante *et al.*, 1997).

Understanding through games

Understanding may also be supported through the use of games. For example, after orienting the children towards the topic in hand, the class could be divided into groups of about four and they could be asked to recall what they already know with a dice game. Each group could be given a sheet of paper, a pencil, a die and each person takes a turn to throw it. They respond to particular tasks according to the number that comes up. Prepare cards with the task lists as follows:

(1) Think of one thing you know about the topic. Write it on the sheet of paper and put a circle around it. Collect one point.
(2) Think of a question you would like to ask about the topic. Write it on the sheet of paper and put a circle around it. Collect two points.
(3) Think of one thing you know about the topic. Write it on the sheet of paper and put a circle around it. Collect one point.
(4) Miss one go.
(5) Think of one thing you know about the topic. Write it on the sheet of paper and put a circle around it. Collect one point.
(6) If there are less than two circles on the paper, miss a turn. If there are two or more circles then think of a way in which any two are connected. Draw a line between the two and write why they are connected along the line. Collect three points.

Each child has one minute to respond to the task. Note that, in this game, one task appears several times. This is to ensure that there is a press for sufficient elements of prior knowledge to enable other tasks to occur.

Card games, domino games, board games – all can be designed to support the making of connections and construction of understanding (Newton, 2001).

Understanding through questions

Teachers often ask a lot of questions at different times and for different purposes. To be worthwhile questions need to be shaped to a particular end (Newton, 1996). This means that the questions asked should support children's thinking at different stages in their understanding. As an example, suppose the aim is for children to understand a situation, such as the way friction makes it difficult to move something. Possible steps in the sequence might be as follows:

* *Orienting children towards the topic*
  Show the children a picture of horses pulling logs from a forest. Ask questions about the picture in general so they tune in to it. Include one or more focused questions, such as, 'What is the horse doing?' 'Does it look easy?' 'Why do you think it looks hard?'

* *Eliciting prior knowledge*
  Move from the first step straight into this one with focused questions of the kind: 'Have you ever tried to pull something along the ground?' 'What was it?' 'Was it hard to do?' 'What do you think made it hard to do?' 'Is there anything that would make it easier?' 'Why does this make it easier?'

* *Developing additional experience*
  On the basis of the children's responses, you may decide that they need additional experience. Have ready a range of surfaces of different thicknesses and some blocks of wood, each with a string attached. The children feel the surfaces to begin with, talk about 'rough', 'smooth', 'catchy' and 'slippy' and look at them with a magnifier. Focused questions during this

time might include: 'Why do you think it is slippy?' 'If the horses had to pull logs over giant sheets of sandpaper like this, would it be hard to do? 'Why?'

- *Making a prediction*
At this point, introduce the wooden blocks. 'We don't have any logs but I've got some wooden blocks. We don't have any horses but we do have you. You can be the horses'. Now ask focused questions like: 'Suppose you were a horse and had to pull your log over these things, which do you think would make it the hardest work?' 'Why do you think that?' 'Which would be the easiest?' 'Why do you think that?' 'So, that's what we think will happen. How can we test our idea?'

- *Planning an experiment*
Focused questions could include: 'What should we do first?' 'Why is it better to do that first?' 'How are we going to make our test fair?' 'Why does that make it fair?' 'Is there anything else we should do to make it fair?' 'How do we know if we are pulling each block with the same pull?' 'Why does that help?'

- *Pulling things together*
Following the practical activity, check that the children have arrived at an adequately founded conclusion. Focused questions might include: 'What were we trying to find out?' 'What did you find?' 'Was it what you expected?' 'So, if we want an easy life, what is it that matters when it comes to dragging things along?'

- *Naming concepts*
Extend the children's vocabulary with the word 'friction'. Focused questions here check for prior knowledge. Ask for examples of how the word is used and have the children use the word in the context of the experiment and horse picture, for example, 'Why do we say this sandpaper gives more friction than that kitchen foil?

- *Applying and extending*
The concept is now applied in new contexts. Focused questions could include: 'Remember that day when it was icy?' 'How many of you fell over?' 'Was that because their was a lot of friction?' 'Why do you say that ice didn't have much friction?' 'What kind of shoes might make it better?' 'Could you have a lot of friction between your shoes and the ice?' 'Why did the caretaker spread sand on the ice?' 'When do we want there to be very little friction. Tell me one time when it would be useful if we did not have a lot of friction'. 'Why is that useful?' 'When would it be useful to have very little friction?' 'Why do we want very little friction on the slide in the playground?' 'Why does it have so little friction against our clothes?

In practice, a teacher might tackle a topic like this in a different way but the point is that, whichever way is chosen, the questions are tailored to each step and are aimed at making the children think about *reasons* for things and *causal links*. One of these focused questions in each cluster is worth a further comment. Asking for a *prediction* is particularly useful because it makes children organise their ideas in order to respond. Their prediction may then be put to the test (applied).

Understanding through bridging

Bridging is a way to link what is to be understood to existing understanding. It may be used when what is to be understood does not immediately relate to anything the children know. It is also useful when what they are to understand is counter-intuitive. In essence, it is the building of a series of mental connections (bridges) from what is known or intuitively accepted to what the teacher wants the children to understand. For example, suppose the goal is for the children to understand what happens to the water in a wet cloth when it dries, that is, the process of evaporation. Evaporation is usually an invisible process and the teacher could end up saying the equivalent of, 'Take my word for it'. It is possible to do more with bridging (Newton, 2001).

First find or arrange something to show evaporation that is reasonably obvi-ous. For example, put out a bowl of warm water on a cold morning. 'Smoke' will be seen coming from the bowl. What is it? Put the bowl close to a cold window. The window will mist over and begin to run with water. The 'smoke' drifts from the dish, onto the window and turns back into water. It is not always possible to see the water leaving the dish. Have the children breathe outside and note their visible 'breath'. Repeated indoors, it is invisible, but it is still there. They test that by breathing on a cold window and see it mist over. What would happen if the dish was left for longer? What happens to puddles in the street? They disappear because the water slowly drifts away. Take a wet cloth and hang it out on a cold day. The water vapour will be seen leaving the cloth. Hold the cloth near the cold window and see the water mist. When water drifts out of things in this way, we say it has evaporated.

The above sequence is, of course, expressed in condensed form and would take a little time to develop. It comprises a bridge from evaporation from a bowl of warm water, to visible and invisible water vapour in breath, to street puddles, to the drying of a wet cloth.

Concluding Comments

Supporting understanding might seem daunting. However, it is unlikely that a teacher would need to invent everything he or she wants to do in a lesson from first principles. Existing resources, such as published materials, and the school science co-ordinator could help. Published materials may not provide all the support for understanding that is wanted but could give ideas for things to do. However, drawing on these, the strategies suggested above could be applied. While supporting understanding can be demanding, it is also very rewarding when a teacher is successful.

Conceptions of what counts as understanding in science and appropriate strate-gies for teaching and learning in primary science are likely to be acquired uncon-sciously. An apprenticeship approach in primary initial teacher training programmes, in which trainees emulate and learn largely from the practices of, for example, a class teacher, risks the learning of weak practices. Further, there seems to be a need for in-service work that is directed towards teaching for understand-ing in science. One problem is that such in-service support can often lead to short-term mental engagement but little long-term translation into practice. Teachers need to be convinced of the worth of teaching for understanding in primary science and supported through the translation. Bandura (1986) argues that teachers with a high level of self-efficacy – a belief that one's actions *can* make a difference – are more likely to put what they know into action. He recommends that self-efficacy be raised using a modelling process. This means that what constitutes a press for and support for understanding should be modelled for teachers. With this as a significant component of both initial and in-service training, primary teachers could learn not only what counts as understanding in primary science, but also how to support its construction.

Correspondence

Any correspondence should be directed to Dr Lynn D. Newton, University of Durham, School of Education, Leazes Road, Durham DH1 1TA, UK (L.D.Newton@durham.ac.uk).

References

Bandura, A. (1986) *Social Foundations of Thought and Action*. New Jersey: Prentice-Hall.

Bruer, J.T. (1994) *Schools for Thought*. Cambridge, MA: MIT Press.

Cavalcante, P.S., Newton, L.D. and Newton, D.P. (1997) The effect of various kinds of lessons on conceptual understanding in science. *Research in Science and Technological Education* 15, 185–193.

Department for Education and Employment [DfEE] (1998) *Teaching: High Status, High Standards* (Circular 4/98: Requirements for Courses of Initial Training Training), London: DfEE/TTA.

Department for Education and Employment [DfEE] (1999) *Science: The National Curriculum for England Key Stages 1–4* London: DfEE/QCA.

Gardner, H. and Boix-Mansilla, V. (1994) Teaching for understanding in the disciplines and beyond. *Teachers College Record* 96, 198–218.

Newton, D.P. (2000) *Teaching for Understanding: What It Is and How To Do It*. London: Routledge-Falmer.

Newton, D.P. (2001) *Talking Sense in Science*. London: Routledge-Falmer.

Newton, D.P. and Newton, L.D. (1995) *A Question of Science*. London: Watts Books.

Newton, D.P. (1998) Enculturation and understanding: Some differences between sixth formers' and graduates' conceptions of understanding. *Teaching in Higher Education* 3, 339–363.

Newton, D.P. (1999) Is primary science taught for understanding? *Studies in Teaching and Learning* 1, 4–11.

Newton, L.D. (1996) Teachers' questioning in primary school science. Unpublished PhD thesis, University of Newcastle-upon-Tyne.

Newton, L.D. (2000) *Meeting the Standards in … Primary Science: A Guide to the ITT NC*. London: Routledge-Falmer.

Nickerson, R.S. (1985) Understanding understanding. *American Journal of Education* 93, 201–239

Piaget, J. (1978) *Success and Understanding*. London: Routledge and Kegan-Paul.

Sierpinska, A. (1994) *Understanding in Mathematics*. London: Falmer Press.

Wildy, H. and Wallace, J. (1992) Understanding teaching or teaching for understanding. *American Educational Research Journal* 29, 143–156.

Developing Young Children's Understanding: An Example from Earth Science

Anthony Blake

University of Newcastle upon Tyne, Department of Education, St Thomas Street, Newcastle upon Tyne NE1 7RU, UK

This paper explores what prior knowledge children from Key Stage 2 (7–11 years) in one school in the north-east of England had of rock classification and how they might develop a more scientific understanding using strategies which have been shown by research to support this process. Strategies chosen were the conceptual model of the rock cycle and the analogy of aluminium can recycling. The children's existing conceptions confirm the findings of earlier research which found that, in contrast with earth scientists, children do not classify rocks on the basis of their origin but instead use simple physical characteristics like hardness and shape. Providing these children with a conceptual model in the form of the rock cycle, particularly when used in conjunction with analogy, had a positive impact on their capacity to classify rocks on the basis of their igneous, sedimentary and metamorphic processes within the rock cycle. However, the role played by the analogy in supporting children's understanding in this domain was difficult to determine with precision. Finally, the importance of recognising that all analogies have their limitations is addressed.

Introduction

In recent revisions of the National Curriculum, the role of Earth Science, in particular its 'geological' dimension, has diminished although it retains its value in terms of increasing children's scientific literacy and as a starting point for scientific investigations. Children also find geology fascinating! (Blake, 1989, 1999). Currently, children in Key Stage 2 (7–11 years old) are required by the National Curriculum to be taught, '… to describe and group rocks and soils on the basis of their characteristics, including appearance, texture and permeability' (DFEE, 1999: 25).

Implicit in this requirement is that children are given the opportunity to develop a scientific understanding of types of rocks and how they are classified. This paper sets out to describe a study of the prior knowledge children in one primary school had of rock classification, and how they might develop a more scientific understanding using strategies which have been shown to support this process.

What Counts as Understanding in Earth Science?

Understanding is self-generated; it is an active cognitive process which enables the individual to establish relationships between relevant, but isolated, pieces of information (Cavalcante *et al.*, 1997). Using the standard picture of cognitive architecture (Bruer, 1993: 23), when faced with a new concept to be understood, existing knowledge from the long-term memory interacts with in-coming information in the working memory to generate a mental representation (Newton, 2000). Children's mental representations however, do not always appear to approximate to a scientific understanding. Research has shown that children have developed alternative ideas or conceptions for a number of concepts in science generally (Driver *et al.*, 1985; Osborne & Freyberg, 1985), and in Earth Science in particular (Happs, 1984; Russell *et al.*, 1993).

Alternative conceptions research has found that young children have a very limited understanding about the Earth's materials. Studies carried out in the United States, New Zealand and the United Kingdom documented the contrast between the scientific view of rocks and their origin, and those of children. Earth scientists describe rocks in terms of their texture and mineral composition, and classify them according to their Igneous, Sedimentary or Metamorphic origin within the conceptual framework of the rock cycle (Duff, 1993; Press & Siever, 1986). In contrast, children used simple physical criteria, such as hardness, shape, weight, colour and smoothness to describe and classify rocks as 'rocks' or 'not rocks' (Happs, 1982, 1984, 1985; Russell *et al.*, 1993). So how might teachers support children's efforts to develop a more scientific understanding of how to classify rocks by their process of formation?

Strategies to Support Understanding in Earth Science

The origin of rocks can be embedded within the conceptual model of the rock cycle to provide what might be termed a 'process-product' view of rocks. The rock cycle itself is often represented as a labelled diagram in standard Earth Science textbooks (Duff, 1993: 32; Press & Siever, 1986: 38). Current cognitive theory suggests that providing conceptual structures, particularly in diagrammatic form (Mayer, 1989), can scaffold children's understanding by reducing processing load (Newton, 2000). Conceptual structures highlight the relevant relationships between concepts that need to be understood (Cavalcante *et al.*, 1997).

Another strategy for supporting understanding in unfamiliar knowledge domains is the use of analogies. Analogies facilitate help in the construction of mental representations and appear useful in displacing more resistant misconceptions held by children (Newton, 2000). Relevant attributes are mapped by the individual child from a familiar to the unfamiliar, more abstract, knowledge domain. A number of factors have been shown to affect analogical learning, including the appropriateness of the analogy employed, and the importance of teaching children explicitly how to use the analogy (Gentner & Gentner, 1983; Newton & Newton, 1995; Zeitoun, 1984). Analogies are not new to learning in Earth Science and have been used to help children understand geological time and sedimentary strata (Hume, 1978; Wagner, 1987). In this study aluminium can recycling was used as an analogy for the rock cycle to assist children in developing a more scientific understanding of the origin of rocks.

The Present Study

Because the classification of rocks can be considered as a network of inter-related concepts (Finley, 1981, 1982), this makes it particularly susceptible to probing using techniques which provide an insight into how children structure their knowledge. The following study was carried out to explore:

- the nature of children's alternative conceptions about how they group rocks and then to compare these with the representations of experts in the field;
- to ascertain the impact of using a conceptual structure and an analogy on children's understanding of the rock cycle.

Method

The sample

Sixty Year 5 and 6 children (9–11 years) from an inner city primary school in the north-east of England were randomly assigned to one of two groups based on the results of a standardised, *Non-Reading Intelligence Test Level 3* (Young, 1973).

Conditions

The two groups were: *Without Analogy (Control) Group*. Children in this group were introduced to the rock cycle in diagrammatic form and shown representative rocks from each part of the rock cycle process. Following discussion, the children were asked to match their table specimens with the correct part of the rock cycle.

With Analogy (Experimental) Group. This group was exposed to analogical teaching using the GMAT model proposed by Zeitoun (1984) as follows. To ensure that they were familiar with analogies, this group was first given an introductory teacher-led lesson on how analogies can be used to help understand unfamiliar topics (Stage A). This was then followed by a lesson about the rock cycle (Stage B). This time the Earth was represented as a dynamic rock recycling machine using the aluminium can recycling process as the functional analogy (Figure 1).

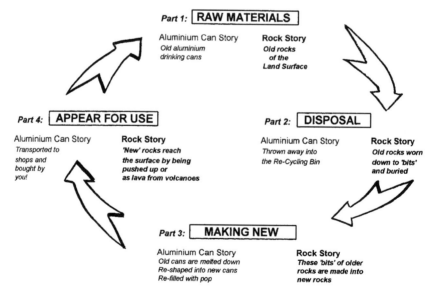

Figure 1 The aluminium can and rock recycling stories compared

Procedure and scoring

All the children were given the same pre-and post-tests which were intended to probe into how they structure their knowledge in terms of the relationship between relevant concepts. The following instruments were used and children were given practice tasks to help familiarise them with the format:

Concept maps provide direct evidence of how children structure their knowledge about rocks, particularly when employing a scoring system which evaluates consistency and accuracy. Concept maps however, are not free from controversy, particularly with regard to how they are scored (Bloom, 1995; Markham *et al.*, 1994; Novak & Gowin, 1984; Novak, 1990; Ruiz-Primo & Shavelson, 1996; Rye & Rubba, 1998; Stuart, 1985; Wandersee, 1990).In this instance pupils' concept maps were scored against a 'master' or 'criterion concept map' since there is a recognised hierarchy of relationships between concepts in respect of classifying rocks by origin in Earth Science. A larger number of valid links which correspond closely with the master concept map are consistent with a richer understanding and vice versa (White & Gunstone, 1992).

Semi-structured interviews were given to 18 children (9 Control, 9 Experimental: 3 above average, 3 average and 3 below average for each group) to provide the flexibility to probe children's understanding in more depth. The interviews incorporated an *Interview-About-Concepts* probe (Abdullah & Scaife, 1997; White & Gunstone, 1992) which allows measurements to made concerning the extent, precision and consistency of a child's knowledge. From the children's responses, matrices of associations between concepts could be constructed as a basis for evaluating pre-and post-intervention performance (White & Gunstone, 1992).

Practical Rock Task (PRT): to lend some variation, as well as triangulation, to the other probes, the children were asked to classify seven representative rock specimens, labelled A to G, from the rock cycle: sandstone (A), granite (B), slate (C), limestone (D), basalt (E), conglomerate (F) and gneiss (G). The children were told they could put the samples into as many or as few groups as they wished, and that each group could have any number of specimens in it. Importantly, the children were told that they must write down beside each group the reason why certain specimens were included.

Results and discussion

The results confirm the findings from earlier research that, in contrast with Earth scientists, the children classified rocks on the basis of simple physical criteria which included shape (30%), colour (33%) and feel (77%). Statistically significant pre-post intervention differences at the 5% level were obtained only for the Analogy Group with regard to the concept map ($p = 0.002$) and the practical rock task ($p = 0.0008$). With regard to the interview-about-concepts probe, neither group's post-intervention *extent* of knowledge score was significantly different, although the Analogy group's *precision* score was ($p = 0.0015$).

How children's understanding changed

On the basis of the triangulated data from all three probes, it was evident that following the intervention, many children's understanding approximated more towards the accepted scientific view of how rocks could be classified on the basis of their origin. Phil, a more able child from the Analogy Group will serve as an example of how children's understanding became more structured, relevant and hierarchically organised, and thus more scientifically accurate.

Whereas before the intervention, Phil classified the specimens in terms of obvious physical criteria, his post-intervention PRT shows that he is now classifying the specimens scientifically, according to their origin (Table 1).

Table 1 Pre-Post criteria used by Phil to classify rocks in the PRT

PRE		POST	
Specimen:	*Criteria*	*Specimen:*	*Criteria*
H	brightly coloured	H	mineral
G	smooth	ADF	Sedimentary
C	dull	BE	Igneous
ABDEF	rough	CG	Metamorphic

Post-intervention, Phil's concept map confirms a re-structuring of his ideas about how rocks are classified. His knowledge of rocks appears to have become increasingly differentiated and hierarchically organised, making it more consistent with the 'master' concept map representation produced by experts in the field (Figure 2).

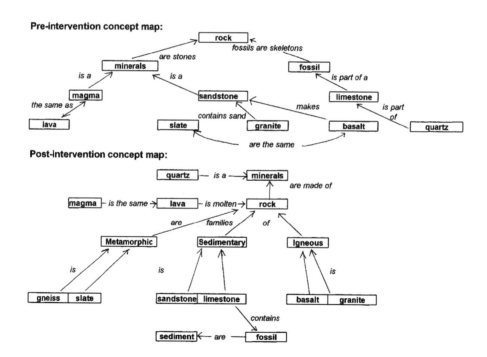

Figure 2 Phil's pre- and post-intervention concept maps

Importantly, Phil has not only re-structured his knowledge of rocks, but he also embedded this within the recycling framework of the rock cycle. This suggests that Phil has a mental representation, possibly in the form of a mental model, of the rock cycle. Witness Phil's interview description of rocks with its implicit knowledge of the rock cycle, and understanding of the derivation of metamorphic rocks from existing rocks:

Interviewer:	Are rocks all the same?
Phil:	No, you get three different families of rocks.
I:	Tell me about that; that sounds interesting.
P:	Sedimentary, metamorphic and igneous.
I:	Why do we have three different families?
P:	Because they are made in different ways.
I:	Can you explain a bit more about that?
P:	Sedimentary are made by bits of other stuff 'clunging' together.
I:	What about metamorphic rocks?
P:	They're made so far down that the rocks get crushed into slate-type rocks … then they push their way up to the surface.
I:	How do they do that?
P:	Pressure under the ground.

For Phil, his interviews-about-concepts responses confirm his understanding of this inter-relationship of these concepts when he discusses the Earth in terms of the recycling of rocks. Association maps of key concepts prior to the intervention show that children from both groups were linking concepts for the most part concerned with land surface features and rocks. However, they omit concepts which relate to the formation of rocks themselves. Post-intervention, besides the richer cross-linking of these existing concepts, Phil's association map of key concepts reveals his new, more integrated, conceptual understanding about the origin of rocks with land surface features (Figure 3).

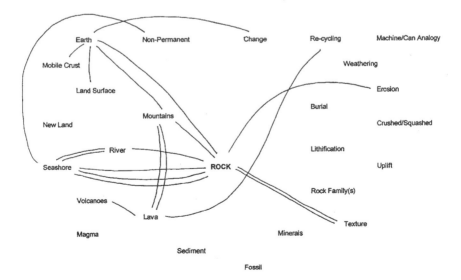

Figure 3a Phil's pre-intervention association map of key concepts

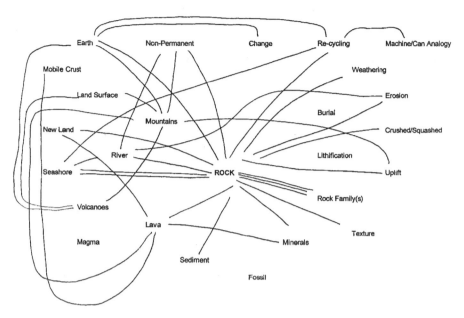

Figure 3b Phil's post-intervention association map of key concepts

The impact of the analogy on the children's understanding

The post-intervention gain scores were more statistically significant for the Analogy Group. Was this a positive effect of the analogy?

The picture is more complex than these differences suggest, and not all children from the Analogy Group did better than the children in the Without Analogy (Control) Group. This indicates that providing children with the analogy was not essential for, or even guaranteed a better, understanding of the rock cycle. For some, the concept of the rock cycle may have been simple enough not to call for an analogy (hence the gains in the Without Analogy Group). Analogy is only effective when the concept is difficult to grasp. It does not seem unreasonable to argue, however, that where the analogy was available, it helped those children who needed it to scaffold their understanding of the rock cycle.

Where the analogy appeared to support understanding

Success of the analogy in supporting children's understanding of the rock cycle is consistent with the transfer of the relevant attributes of the analogue, with the absence, or minimum amount, of misconceptions arising from the transfer of irrelevant attributes (Zeitoun, 1984). Recognising how potentially more effective analogical learning can be when mapping between source and target is made explicit (Arnold & Millar, 1996), the intervention had stressed the correspondence between the relevant attributes. It also highlighted those aspects, for example of time scale, human involvement and nature of the product, which were irrelevant, and which might generate misconceptions. Therefore, the intervention did not rely on children *spontaneously* mapping between source and target. Without exception, all interviewees in the Analogy Group referred to the analogy, as their association maps of key concepts confirm. They were able to recognise, and discuss, relevant and irrelevant attributes, which suggests that the analogy had the potential to be effective in supporting their understanding.

However, it is difficult to say with precision *who* actually used the analogy in the Analogy Group and *how* they used it. Possibly, it was used as an aid to thought, and as we only see the products of such thought, and not the process, we do not have evidence of the analogy being used to process a response. Children in the Analogy Group who were interviewed did not furnish spontaneous, detailed explanations of the rock cycle, drawing on analogies to assist in their account. As found in other studies (Newton & Newton, 1995), the children required continuous prompting and reminding about the analogy, and in describing both relevant and irrelevant attributes. Possibly some children may either not have needed to use the analogy in the first place, or after employing the analogy at the point of instruction to support their understanding, it was no longer required, becoming an unwelcome complication in structuring their response to the interview question.

Where analogy failed to support understanding

The analogy might be said to have 'failed', where children exposed to it were unable to demonstrate a good understanding of the rock cycle. This may have been due to a range of factors which, besides more personal student characteristics, include:

- that the analogy was, for some children, unnecessary as we have noted above;
- that the analogy had certain limitations in terms of not impacting on all the areas of understanding needed to develop complete mental representations.

Some children showed an understanding of the rock cycle, but for some reason did not classify rocks by origin as their concept map showed. The answer most logically would seem to lie in the fact that the analogy itself did not *directly* relate to this aspect of understanding. That is, in helping children classify particular rocks by origin from their textural clues. There were no analogous attributes in the source which corresponded to metamorphic, sedimentary or igneous processes, although her interview responses point to a more general understanding that *all* rocks were formed by recycling within the rock cycle framework itself. Newton and Newton (1995) discovered similar limitations in the application of a water circuit analogy to an electric current. All analogies have their restrictions and will not help all children acquire all the attributes of the target domain (Heywood & Parker, 1997; Zeitoun, 1984). Therefore, while the aluminium can analogy may have proved useful in developing an overall mental representation of the rock cycle, its impact on some children's ability to classify rocks by origin was only *indirect*. The analogy facilitated an understanding of the rock cycle, which in turn may have 'forced' some of the children to view rocks in this manner.

Conclusions

This study set out to establish the nature of children's existing ideas about rock classification and the impact of providing two strategies to support children's development of a more scientific understanding.

Pre-intervention probes confirmed the difference in the structuring of knowl-edge relating to the classification of rocks between children and Earth scientists. Following the intervention, 31 children (52%) demonstrated a capacity to classify rocks by origin. This appears to be a direct consequence of children's exposure to the conceptual model of the rock cycle. The rock cycle provided an integrated framework which encouraged children to construct a mental representation of the rock cycle. This promotes a more scientific process-product view of rocks in contrast with a consideration of rocks in the more limited terms of their physical characteristics. The provision of a rock cycle structure alone, however, did not guarantee that children would be able to sort rocks in this way. Not all children who showed a good grasp of the rock cycle were able to classify rocks in terms of their processes of formation. It may be that the processing demand of this conceptual model, which involves the classification of rocks in terms of their processes of formation, was simply too great for some of the children.

Although there were no analogous attributes to cover specific processes, the analogy seems to have facilitated indirectly an understanding of *related* concepts, in this study shown by children's capacity to classify rocks in terms of their origin. Thus if the analogy is of value in helping some children develop an under-standing of the dynamic Earth through the rock cycle then *ipso facto*, it must, indi-rectly, facilitate an understanding of how rocks are grouped by origin. However, while this study has confirmed how useful analogies can be in supporting under-standing, it is important for teachers to recognise that all analogies have their limitations. For some children in the study, the analogy appears not to have provided support they needed. Considerable care is required in finding suitable analogies.

Correspondence

Any correspondence should be directed to Dr Anthony Blake, University of Newcastle, Department of Education, St Tomas Street, Newcastle Upon Tyne NE1 7RU, UK (Anthony.Blake@ncl.ac.uk).

References

Abdullah, A. and Scaife, J. (1997) Using interviews to assess children's understanding of science concepts. *School Science Review* 78 (285), 79–83.

Arnold, M. and Millar, R. (1996) Exploring the use of analogy in the teaching of heat, temperature and thermal equilibrium. In G. Welford, J. Osborne and P. Scott (eds) *Research in Science Education in Europe: Current Issues and Themes*. London: Falmer.

Blake, A. (1989) Running a school geology club. *Primary Science Review* 9, 9–11.

Blake, A. (1999) Children's understanding of aspects of Earth science at Key Stage 2: Conceptions and conceptual change. Unpublished Ed.D. thesis University of Newcastle Upon Tyne.

Bloom, J.W. (1995) Assessing and extending the scope of children's contexts of meaning: Context maps as a methodological perspective *International Journal of Science Education* 17 (2), 167–187.

Bruer, J.T. (1993) *Schools for Thought*. Cambridge: MIT Press.

Cavalcante, P.S., Newton, D.P. and Newton, L.D. (1997) The effect of various kinds of lesson on conceptual understanding in science *Research in Science and Technological Education* 15 (2), 185–193.

DFEE (1999) *Science Key Stages 1–4*. London: HMSO.

Driver, R., Guesne, E. and Tiberghien, A. (eds) (1985) *Children's Ideas in Science*. Buckingham: Open University Press.

Duff, D. (1993) *Holmes' Principles of Physical Geology* (4th edn). London: Chapman and Hall.

Finley, F.N. (1981) A philosophical approach to describing science content: An example from geologic classification. *Science Education* 65 (5), 513–519.

Finley, F.N. (1982) An empirical determination of concepts contributing to successful performance of a science process: A study of mineral classification. *Journal of Research in Science Teaching* 19 (8), 689–696.

Gentner, D. and Gentner, D.R. (1983) Flowing waters or teeming crowds: Mental models of electricity. In Gentner and Stevens (eds) *Mental Models*. Hillsdale, NJ: Lawrence Erlbaum.

Happs, J.C. (1982) Rocks and minerals. *Science Education Research Unit Working Paper No. 204*. New Zealand: Waikato University.

Happs, J.C. (1984) The utility of alternative knowledge frameworks in effecting conceptual change: Some examples from the Earth sciences. Unpublished D.Phil thesis, University of Waikato, New Zealand.

Happs, J.C. (1985) Regression on learning outcomes: Some examples from the Earth sciences. *European Journal of Science Education* 7 (4), 431–443.

Heywood, D. and Parker, J. (1997) Confronting the analogy: Primary teachers exploring the usefulness of analogies in the teaching and learning of electricity. *International Journal of Science Education* 19 (8), 869–885.

Hume, J.D. (1978) An understanding of geologic time. *Journal of Geological Education* 26, 141–143.

Markham, K.M., Mintzes, J.J. and Jones, M.G. (1994) The concept map as a research tool: Further evidence of validity. *Journal of Research in Science Teaching* 31 (1), 91–101.

Mayer, R.E. (1989) Systematic thinking fostered by illustrations in scientific text. *Journal of Educational Psychology* 81 (2), 240–246.

Newton, D.P. and Newton, L.D. (1995) Using analogy to help young children understand. *Educational Studies* 21 (3), 379–393.

Newton, D.P. (2000) *Teaching for Understanding*. London: Routledge Falmer.

Novak, J.D. and Gowin, D.B. (1984) *Learning How to Learn*. Cambridge: Cambridge University Press.

Novak, J.D. (1990) Concept mapping: A useful tool for science education. *Journal of Research in Science Teaching* 27 (10), 937–949.

Osborne, R. and Freyberg, P. (eds) (1985) *Learning in Science: The Implications of 'Children's Science'*. London: Heinemann.

Press, F. and Siever, R. (1986) *Earth* (4th edn). New York: W.H.Freeman and Co.

Ruiz-Primo, M.A. and Shavelson, R.J. (1996) Problems and issues in the use of concept maps in science assessment. *Journal of Research in Science Teaching* 33 (6), 569–600.

Russell, T., Bell, D., Longden, K. and McGuigan, L. (1993) *Primary SPACE Research Report: Rocks, Soil and Weather*. Liverpool: Liverpool University Press.

Rye, J.A. and Rubba, P.A. (1998) An exploration of the concept map as an interview tool to facilitate the externalization of students' understanding about global atmospheric change. *Journal of Research in Science Teaching* 35, 521–546.

Stuart, H.A. (1985) Should concept maps be scored numerically? *European Journal of Science Education* 7 (1), 73–81.

Wagner, J.R. (1987) Using layer cake geology to illustrate structural topographic relationships. *Journal of Geological Education* 35, 33–36.

Wandersee, J.H. (1990) Concept mapping and the cartography of cognition. *Journal of Research in Science Teaching* 27 (10), 923–936.

White, R. and Gunstone, R. (1992) *Probing Understanding*. London: Falmer Press.

Young, D. (1973) *Non-Reading Intelligence Tests Levels 1–3*. London: Hodder and Stoughton.

Zeitoun, H.H. (1984) Teaching scientific analogies: A proposed model. *Research in Science and Technological Education* 2 (2), 107–125.

ICT and Teaching for Understanding

Steve Higgins
Department of Education, University of Newcastle upon Tyne, St Thomas Street,
Newcastle upon Tyne NE1 7RU, UK

Steve Higgins
Department of Education, University of Newcastle upon Tyne, St Thomas Street,
Newcastle upon Tyne NE1 7RU, UK

This article considers some of the possibilities of the ways in which Information and Communications Technology (ICT) can support teaching for understanding in primary schools. Drawing on research analysed for a Teacher Training Agency (TTA) study and work in progress in the North East of England supporting ICT training for serving teachers in England it suggests that there are clear possibilities for improving learners' understanding using ICT. However, there are also limitations, such as pupils' access to ICT, teachers' beliefs and knowledge of their subjects and their ICT skills as well as the rapid changes in technology itself, all of which make it difficult for these possibilities to be assimilated effectively.

Introduction

In this article the role and potential of Information and Communications Technology (ICT) in effective teaching and in developing learners' understanding will be considered, drawing on the literature review and then the research and development work conducted for a Teacher Training Agency (TTA) funded project *Effective Pedagogy Using ICT for Literacy and Numeracy in Primary Schools* (Moseley *et al.*, 1999). It also includes reference to work undertaken at the University of Newcastle developing materials and approaches for a New Opportunities Fund (NOF) ICT course *Thinking Through Literacy Numeracy and Science*, delivered by GridREF 2000, an approved training provider based in the North East of England.

The UK government has invested considerable sums in information and communications technology in education through the 'National Grid for Learning', which aims to create an effective infrastructure, and through the £230 million investment of National Lottery money in ICT training for serving teachers. The outcomes for this training (TTA, 1999) emphasise the importance of teachers' understanding of ICT and its 'significant' … 'potential for improving the quality of pupils' learning'.

ICT is both a subject in the National Curriculum (DfEE, 1999) for England and Wales and a complex tool which can be used by teachers and by pupils in teaching and learning. This makes the approach in this article different from the others in this collection. My intention is to look at ICT as a tool and the evidence for how it can contribute to the development of understanding across the curriculum, rather than the development of understanding of pupils of ICT as a subject within the curriculum.

Understanding is the theme for this Special Edition of ERIE, and others in the collection have considered some of the issues in defining and grappling with this term. My starting point is a simpler one, and, at the risk of being simplistic, is based on Dewey's definition 'To understand is to grasp meaning' (Dewey, 1933: 132). My intention is to consider how ICT can help pupils' in deriving meaning through teaching activities and how pupils use of ICT can support them in making their learning meaningful. The examples are drawn mainly from mathematics teaching and learning in primary schools (5–11 years). This is in part due to the need to focus on one particular area for this article, and partly because the use of ICT in mathematics has tended to be polarised between skills teaching, such as drill and practice or more sophisticated Integrated Learning Systems (ILS) and constuctivism-led approaches, such as LOGO (Higgins & Mujis, 1999). This polarity offers an insight into the issue of understanding.

Dewey elaborates upon his definition of understanding with a typically pragmatic extension:

> To grasp the meaning of a thing, an event or a situation is to see it in its *relations* to other things: to note how it operates or functions, what consequences follow from it, what causes it, what uses it can be put to. (Dewey, 1933: 137)

This immediately identifies an issue when applied to the use of ICT, particularly in primary schools where studies suggest that there is little actual computer use by pupils and that such use is usually unconnected with other teaching and learning activities. Drill and practice and typing up of 'a best copy' are often the prevalent activities (Chalkey & Nicholas, 1997). The update of the ORACLE project (Galton *et al.*, 1999) conducted a large number of observations in primary classrooms between 1996 and 1997. Of almost 1000 pupil observations only 12 involved pupils using ICT. The authors do note that their sampling method may have under-represented the actual time pupils use ICT as they focused on individuals. However, it still suggests overall use by pupils was very low. Evidence is not yet available about how the implementation of the National Literacy and Numeracy Strategies and the investment in new equipment are altering patterns of use. Anecdotally the impression is that drill and practice, or typing up of work has been replaced in some schools with the direct teaching of painting and word-processing skills on clusters of computers, but that direct teaching in other areas of the curriculum is still rare. In the TTA study teachers reported the least usage of ICT for direct teaching (Moseley *et al.*, 1999: 83). Again there is no evidence to date that it is becoming more frequent. The use of ICT in primary schools is still likely to be discrete skills teaching and where links to other learning are not made. The current opportunities for developing understanding through such use are therefore limited. There is simply not much opportunity for learning through ICT or for making connections where any do occur with other teaching and learning in school.

The Literature Background

One of the inferences drawn from the research base analysed for the TTA project was that ICT was powerful in presenting or representing information in different ways (e.g. Ainsworth *et al.*, 1997). This might be through speech and text, or text and pictures for literacy and pictures and numerals or through tables and graphs for mathematics.

ICT clearly also has potential to represent information dynamically so that the learner can make changes easily. This can support evaluation and understanding of those changes either in one representation (e.g. editing text in word-processing (Breese *et al.*, 1996; Snyder, 1993) and observing changes and patterns in spreadsheets (Mann & Tall, 1992) or between representations (e.g. tabulated and visual data (Ainsworth *et al.*, 1997)).

The research reviewed for the TTA project indicated that when researchers initiated ICT activities for pupils they tended to use computer assisted instruction or computer assisted learning software where learning content was presented to pupils. Such studies can perhaps be characterised as testing learning theory, particularly from a psychological perspective (Moseley *et al.*, 1999: viii). The focus of these projects was to identify measurable gain in pupil performance, usually on the basis of skills testing. By contrast, when teachers carried out action research, their preferred choice was more open ended or generic software. They reported positively about the benefits for pupils but with the consequence that such studies were rarely linked with pupil outcome data. As a result of this apparent dichotomy, gains have been hard to attribute directly to the use of ICT, and there is little to indicate that ICT can bring about improvements in terms of understanding. Gains tended to be in reading (particularly decoding skills), in spelling or in numerical skills.

Teachers' Thinking, ICT and Pupil Outcomes

There is also evidence that teachers' thinking affects their choices about how to use ICT and that these patterns of preference are associated with the learning gains that their pupils make (Higgins & Moseley, 2001). In work developing out of the TTA study constructs about teaching and learning were elicited from teachers of Reception (4–5 year olds), Year 2 (6–7 year olds) and Year 4 (8–9 year olds). Ranking of constructs relating to ICT and learning were compared with pupil performance data, questionnaire information about classroom practice and teachers' self-reports of ICT skills and confidence. Internally consistent patterns of thinking were found for the group of 75 teachers. There were some clear differences that emerged according to the year group that the teachers taught in the way these patterns predicted pupil progress. Teachers' attitudes towards ICT and ways of using it were significantly linked with pupil outcomes in literacy and numeracy. Similarly there were links between the way teachers reported that they used computers and the relative pupil progress data from the Performance Indicators in Primary Schools project (PIPS) based at Durham University. For Reception teachers a degree of scepticism about the value of ICT and purposeful use of computers was a positive indicator of pupils' progress. Teachers of Year 2 pupils who valued more open-ended tasks, favoured ICT (though were selective in how they used it) and favoured exciting teaching were likely to be more effective. For teachers of Year 4 the use of ICT for demonstration and purposeful use by pupils as well as a teacher direction dimension were associated with pupils' progress. Whilst this study was relatively small, it indicates that the different beliefs and choices of teachers are likely to affect pupils' learning in different ways, even within the years of the primary school.

ICT and Mathematics

The emphasis in the research literature about ICT and mathematics is on CAI (Computer Assisted Instruction) or CAL (Computer Aided Learning) and mainly reports studies of secondary or post-secondary mathematics teaching and learning. Overall the benefit reported by these studies is relatively low and computer use has not generally found to be as effective as other approaches such as peer tutoring or homework. There is very little research specifically on primary mathematics, still fewer empirical studies containing information on pupils' understanding of number. Where such studies are reported they are often on intervention studies with a specific and precise learning goal rather than improving mathematical understanding more generally.

Integrated Learning Systems (ILS), offer plenty of appropriate examples for pupils to practise and provide feedback to pupils on screen and to teachers through reports of errors made. The preliminary evaluations of ILS suggested that they were not particularly beneficial for pupils aged 5–7 years though early indications suggested that they might be more effective for older pupils. The final evaluation (Wood, 1998) indicated that, at least for pupils aged 11–14, the ILS systems evaluated were not effective in raising attainment in mathematics, although they might possibly be helpful for remediation or as a 'catch up' solution, particularly for lower attaining pupils. The issue, particularly for higher attaining pupils, was that the approaches did not seem to support the learning of new ideas and understanding in mathematics.

Current new software tends to concentrate on developing specific number skills, particularly addition and multiplication facts, following an approach which can crudely be characterised as inspired by a behaviourist approach to learning. Problems or questions are presented to pupils by the computer. The computer then provides a reward of some kind (a score or a positive sound) if they provide a correct solution. Research on assessment suggests that feedback may not help them to improve (Black & Wiliam, 1998). Pupils learn to subvert the system through any help available (Balacheff & Kaput, 1996) and treat tasks as computer games where 'cheats' are an accepted part of the process.

On the other hand, constructivist or understanding-led approaches to software design have not been able to claim much success in raising attainment in mathematics either. LOGO is perhaps the premier example in this area. Much was claimed for this innovative programming language, which enabled very young children to develop mathematical ideas through the use of precise language. However, the evidence of impact on pupils' mathematical attainment has been disappointing in this area too (Yelland, 1995).

The use of portable computers and palmtops has also been investigated. Some results have been encouraging. The use of such machines can clearly have a beneficial impact on children's mathematical thinking (e.g. Ainley & Pratt, 1995). The issue here is how the machines are used. Projects like this involve considerable development work with teachers and have usually taken a constructivist approach to learning for both the teachers and the pupils. Ainley and Pratt describe the development of teachers' mathematical understanding as well as the development of their technical expertise. In addition, such development work saw the particular hardware and software as mathematical tools for pupils to use, rather than seeing the technology itself as a teaching tool.

Clearly related to the issue of the way teachers approach the use of hardware and software is the difficulty teachers find in using some open-ended programs effectively. A person's understanding of mathematics limits what they see as the potential for use of a program as Bradshaw (1993) reports about Numerator. It can also be harder to organise the use of such programs in the classroom and in some instances they may take longer or be more challenging to learn how to use. These reasons perhaps explain the limited use of approaches and programs of this type. The implication for schools is that effective teaching using such approaches requires investment in both ICT training for teachers and investment in professional development in mathematics.

Taken together, the evidence from these different approaches to using ICT in primary mathematics suggests that to develop understanding the teacher is needed to mediate the learning from ICT activities. It is this mediation which helps them understand how the specific learning 'connects' to other mathematical activities. Askew *et al.* (1997) found that such 'connectionist teachers' were more effective at teaching primary mathematics. The implication is therefore that use of ICT to develop understanding will require a careful pedagogical match between the specific goals of a lesson, the ICT and how it is used, then the way this learning is made meaningful or 'bridged' by the teacher.

ICT as a Catalyst

Further evidence that the pedagogy is as important as the technology comes from work undertaken by Wegerif *et al.* (1998) at the Open University. In this research an approach has been developed using computers that prepares children to work effectively together with specially designed computer-based activities focused on curriculum-related topics. A series of 'Talk Lessons' are followed, in which classes establish ground-rules for collaboration such as listening with respect, responding to challenges with reasons, encouraging partners to give their views and trying to reach agreement. These activities are not only concerned with improving the quality of children's working relationships, but also with developing their use of language as a tool for reasoning and constructing knowledge. That is, the Talk Lessons encourage teachers to create a 'community of enquiry' in their classrooms in which children are guided in their use of language as a tool for both individual reasoning and collaborative problem-solving. Computers are used not only for stimulating effective language use but also for focusing children's joint activity on curriculum tasks. This embedded and catalytic role for computers in primary education is distinctive (Wegerif, 1996; Wegerif & Scrimshaw, 1997; Wegerif *et al.*, 1998).

The evaluations of the Talk Lessons programmes have shown that computer-based activities can be used to stimulate reasoned discussion *and* focus joint activity on curriculum-related learning and that the increased use of explicit, reasoned discussion improves children's individual scores on a test of reasoning (the Raven's Progressive Matrices test). This is persuasive evidence that the use of ICT can support the development of understanding.

Issues

In summary, the evidence available indicates that ICT can support teaching for understanding, but that this is a complex process. Certain features or functions of ICT (TTA, 1999) may well lend themselves to supporting effective demonstration by the teacher, facilitate changing and evaluating information either by the teacher or by pupils, or support communication of ideas. The impact of the use of such technology will depend upon the context of how the ICT is used and the teacher's skill in making the connections meaningful with learners. If Dewey is correct then this will also require active participation on the part of learners:

> things gain meaning when they are used as means to bring about consequences,... or as standing for consequences for which we have to discover means. The relation of means-consequence is the center and heart of all understanding'. (Dewey, 1933: 146)

Of course, ICT will also have an impact on the nature of the curriculum itself. To date there is little evidence that the latest revision of the National Curriculum in England and Wales has grappled with how ICT might change the nature of what we plan to teach in schools, outside of ICT as a separate subject. Two examples may perhaps make the point. In mathematics, graphical solutions to algebraic equations have traditionally been taught as alternatives after basic algebra. Programmes, like Cabri Geomètre, which enable easy manipulation, are visually compelling and may lead to changes in the order of what it is effective to teach. In communication, the issue of visual literacy may become so compelling that new subjects and new understandings will emerge. We may retrench from a strongly symbolic to a more iconic system of meanings. However, the resistance to curriculum change is a historical fact, and ICT may be compelled to support retrospective pedagogies rather than support the prospective and emerging pedagogies across the curriculum (Higgins & Moseley, 2001). Teaching for understanding using ICT is therefore always likely to be a challenging prospect, as others have recently argued (see, for example, the collection of chapters on ICT pedagogy and the curriculum in Loveless & Ellis, 2001).

Conclusion

Understanding does not necessarily occur automatically. Teaching for understanding will always require active assessment from teachers about the meaning that pupils derive from the different educational activities that they engage in so that they can make effective choices about how to develop (or induct pupils into) the shared meanings and understandings that constitute the various subjects of the curriculum. Understanding requires active construction on the part of pupils:

> There is a challenge to understanding only when there is a desired consequence to which means have to be found by inquiry, or things (including symbols in the degree in which experience has matured) are presented under conditions where reflection is required to see what consequences can be effected by their use. (Dewey, 1933: 147)

Personally, I believe that the development of such understanding is not a process of increasingly abstract constructions which can be considered decontextualised, but rather successive recontextualisations of experience (Walkerdine, 1988). ICT offers the opportunity to extend and develop and experiment with such recontextualisations in a purposeful context, so that ideas can be reshaped and developed quickly and easily in different forms using the multi-media capabilities of ICT.

ICT can manipulate, present and exchange information and ideas in different forms, quickly and easily. It is a tool that can be used by teachers for this purpose in their teaching so that the relationship between ideas can be highlighted and explored. Pupils can also benefit form this tool by exploring these ideas for themselves and their consequences as they see, listen and experiment with these ideas purposefully. It is an essential tool for developing understanding. The challenge for research is to identify more systematically the ways that it can support the development of pupils' understanding effectively in the range of social and curriculum contexts in schools. The current pace of technological change may make this task impossible.

Correspondence

Any correspondence should be directed to Steve Higgins, Department of Education, University of Newcastle upon Tyne, St Thomas Street, Newcastle upon Tyne NE1 7RU, UK (s.e.higgins@ncl.ac.uk).

References

Ainley, J. and Pratt, D. (1995) Planning for portability: Integrating mathematics and technology in the primary curriculum. In L. Burton and B. Jaworski (eds) *Technology in Mathematics Teaching* (pp. 435–448) Lund: Chartwell-Bratt.

Ainsworth, S.E., Bibby, P.A. and Wood, D.J. (1997) Information technology and multiple representations: New opportunities – new problems. *Journal of Information Technology for Teacher Education* 6, 93–106.

Askew, M., Brown, M., Rhodes, V., Johnson, D. and Wiliam, D. (1997) *Effective Teachers of Numeracy Final Report.* London: King's College.

Balacheff, N. and Kaput, J.J. (1996) Computer-based learning environments in mathematics. In A.J. Bishop, K. Clements, C. Keitel, J. Kilpatrick and C. Laborde (eds) *International Handbook of Mathematics Education.* Dordrecht: Kluwer Academic Publishers.

Black, P. and Wiliam, D. (1998) *Inside the Black Box: Raising Standards Through Classroom Assessment.* London: Kings College.

Bradshaw, J. (ed.) (1993) *Numerator in the Mathematics Classroom.* Leicester: The Mathematical Association.

Breese, C., Jackson, A. and Prince, T. (1996) Promise in impermanence: Children writing with unlimited access to word processors. *Early Child Development and Care* 118, 67–91.

Chalkey, T.W. and Nicholas, D. (1997) Teacher's use of information technology: Observations of primary school practice. *Aslib Proceedings* 49, 97–107.

Department for Education and Employment (1999) *The National Curriculum.* London: HMSO Publications.

Dewey, J. (1933) *How We Think.* Boston: Heath and Comp.

Galton, G., Hargreaves, L., Comber, C. and Pell, A. (1999) *Inside the Primary Classroom 20 Years On.* London: Routledge.

Higgins, S. and Moseley, D. (2001) Teachers' thinking about ICT and learning: Beliefs and outcomes. *Teacher Development* 5 (2), 191–210.

Higgins, S. and Mujis, D. (1999) ICT and numeracy in primary schools. In I. Thompson (ed.) *Issues in Teaching Numeracy in Primary Schools.* Buckingham: Open University Press.

Loveless, A. and Ellis, V. (2001) *ICT, Pedagogy and the Curriculum: Subject to Change.* London: Routledge Falmer.

Mann, W. J.A. and Tall, D. (eds) (1992) *Computers in the Mathematics Curriculum.* London: The Mathematical Association.

Moseley, D., Higgins, S., Bramald, R., Hardman, F., Miller, J., Mroz, M., Tse, H., Newton, D., Thompson, I., Williamson, J., Halligan, J., Bramald, S., Newton, L., Tymms, P. Henderson, B. and Stout, J. (1999) *Ways Forward with ICT: Effective Pedagogy Using Information and Communications Technology in Literacy and Numeracy in Primary Schools.* Newcastle upon Tyne: University of Newcastle upon Tyne.

Teacher Training Agency (1999) *The Use of ICT in Subject Teaching: Expected Outcomes for ICT Training.* London: Department for Education and Employment.

Snyder, I. (1993) Writing with word processors: A research overview. *Educational Research* 35, 49–68.

Walkerdine, V. (1988) *The Mastery of Reason.* London: Routledge.

Wegerif, R. (1996) Using computers to help coach exploratory talk across the curriculum. *Computers and Education* 26 (1–3), 51–60.

Wegerif, R. and Scrimshaw, P. (eds) (1997) *Computers and Talk in the Primary Classroom.* Clevedon: Multilingual Matters.

Wegerif, R., Mercer, N. and Dawes, L. (1998) Integrating pedagogy and software design to support discussion in the primary curriculum. *Journal of Computer Assisted Learning* 14, 199–211

Wood, D. (1998) *The UK ILS Evaluations: Final Report.* Coventry: BECTA/DfEE.

Yelland, N. (1995) Mindstorms or storm in a teacup? A review of research with LOGO. *International Journal of Mathematical Education for Science and Technology* 26, 853–869.

Teaching for Understanding in Primary Geography

John Halocha
Senior Lecturer in Primary Education, Bishop Grosseteste College, Lincoln LN1 3DY, UK

Geography as a National Curriculum subject, like other foundation subjects, has tended to be marginalised because of the push to raise standards in literacy and numeracy and the emphasis for assessment of the core curriculum areas. Yet an understanding of the world constructed through the study of geography has much to offer the primary age child. In this paper, what is meant by understanding in geography is discussed and the place of geography in current curriculum legislation considered. Finally, some strategies teachers might use to support children in the development of their geographical understanding are provided.

Introduction

> Of course the first thing to do was to make a grand survey of the country she was going to travel through. 'It's something very like learning geography', thought Alice, as she stood on tiptoe in hopes of being able to see a little further'. (Carroll, 1872)

Alice clearly knew the importance of understanding her world. However, the world in which the present generation of primary school pupils live is very different. On the one hand children today have access to an increasingly wide range of geographical information at second-hand through developments in information technology. On the other hand, changes in society lead many pupils to have more restricted first-hand experiences of the world (Hillman, 1993) than perhaps were available to Alice in her time. Jameson (1991) describes it as 'a world where electronically generated images prevail ... a world which is increasingly difficult to touch or tie down'. The aim of this article is to critically discuss the possible nature of primary pupils' geographical understanding as we move into a new and challenging century. The first section will examine various perspectives on what counts as understanding in geography. The second section will place this within the context of current curriculum legislation and 'official' guidelines. Finally, ways in which teachers can support children in the development of their geographical understanding will be discussed.

What Counts as Understanding in Geography?

> By the time they go to school most children have acquired some awareness of the world around them and have begun to form a notion of their own identity within it. (Smeaton, 1998)

The variety of experiences of the world which pupils bring with them to school provide a strong starting point for discussing geographical understanding. They will all have experienced various ways of travelling around, ranging from walking in their locality to aircraft journeys around the world. They will have met many different people who do different jobs and live in many different ways. They will have experienced change in the seasons and have interacted with parts of the physical world such as streams and hills. They will have heard adults talking about distant people and places and perhaps begun to have formed images of these in their own minds. They will have watched television programmes from many countries and had varying exposure to a wide range of images and values from other types of media. They may have been told not to drop litter or seen adults taking items to re-cycling points. They eat food and own toys from many places around the world. They may have favourite places such as a den at the bottom of the garden and may also be frightened of others like the derelict house they pass on the way to school. They may have experienced change in the world, for example the loss of a field they once played in when new homes are built on it. But all of these experiences are random and apparently unrelated to the young mind. What may we define as geographical understanding which will help pupils make sense of these constantly growing experiences?

> Strategies are sought that will make it possible for teachers and students to work with and as enquirers to confront their own notions and ideas about the way the world works and about the meaning of teaching and learning as a process rather than mere knowledge acquisition. (Hart & Nolan, 1999)

Geographical enquiry is central to effective understanding. Children need opportunities to ask geographical questions, learn various ways of observing the world and recording their findings, develop their own views and opinions of their findings and be able to communicate them effectively. Within this enquiry process, they also need opportunities to learn to interpret their finding and offer explanations. Catling (1998) argues that 'the best learning occurs when children are encouraged and challenged to offer their own explanations'. They could be encouraged to give reasons why their old playing field was built on and in so doing the need to collect information and make decisions based upon it.

A sense of scale is crucial to geographical understanding but not just in the way it is used in maps. 'Geographers deal with a local-global dialectic' (Johnson *et al.*, 1995). On the one hand pupils need to develop an understanding of their immediate surrounding but gradually be given opportunities to see how they fit into broader global patterns. For instance, they have to dispose of their fast-food container from a global chain of shops, but so do thousands of other children around the world: this raises sustainability issues both at a local and global scale.

Closely linked to the concept of scale is the need to understand the importance of cause and effect at a range of scales and to understand geographical patterns and relationships. For instance, if forests on the hillsides in St Lucia are cut down and replaced with banana plantations, the tropical rains wash huge amounts of soil into the sea, which in turn affects the ecosystems in the coral reefs just off the coast. However, bananas are a crucial part of the economy and land on the island is in short supply. This type of enquiry will most likely be done with secondary sources, but if a similar environmental issue can be found locally pupils will begin to understand geographical patterns and relationships around the world. For example, the effects of a local landfill site would provide a cogent means of developing their understanding that similar issues and debates occur across the world.

It is also important to distinguish the difference between geographical patterns and processes in developing their understanding of their world. Patterns exist in many forms, for instance in regional variations of temperature across the United Kingdom or the street layouts used by architects during various decades of the 20th century. Processes are the series of events which cause changes in an environment: A river gradually meandering across a flood plain is such an example, as is the migration of peoples from areas of increasing drought.

Patterns and processes also require a time dimension to be integrated within pupils' geographical understanding. Again, a flexible sense of scale is also important: a flash flood can change an environment and people's way of life overnight. We can only begin to understand how a river erodes its channel and meanders across the landscape, eroding, transporting and depositing its load if we can develop some sense of the thousands of years this may take. At the largest scale of all, many adults find it hard to comprehend the huge timescales involved in geological change and the formation of rocks and fossils. Computer simulations and graphics can go some way in helping children to understand the important effects of time on spatial activities.

> When the time dimension is added, then changing structures take on added gleam. (Haggett, 1990)

Understanding the important effects of time can be extended into geographical work using the concept of 'futures education' (Hicks, 1994). In these activities they are encouraged to think of their own futures, gradually moving out to their community and finally possible futures at a global scale. A key element in this process is helping children understand they can have control over some aspects of the future, enabling them to consider and justify their ideas. Futures education can also support their understanding of PSHE and citizenship on a continuum from local to global scales.

Time also affects the geographical tools used in geographical enquiry and it is important that children begin to understand how these may affect our understanding of the world. In the past, it was not until complex navigational skills were developed alongside accurate instruments such as ship-borne timepieces that explorers were able to travel and accurately map the world. Technological developments continue to change the ways in which we can describe, understand and predict change in the world. Haggett (1990) argues that 'mapping is likely to change from a ROM to a RAM format'. By this he means that whereas traditional maps and atlases had their contents fixed and out-of date as soon as they were printed, access to modern computer mapping and Geographical Information Systems enables us to ask new questions and solve complex spatial problems, for example in modelling and predicting the spread of disease on a global scale, through being able to select and manipulate the geographical data held on computer maps. With advances in these technologies growing rapidly, it will be crucial for children to understand the opportunities and issues surrounding them.

Children's geographical understanding can be extended through the active application of thinking skills. In this way 'children can focus on knowing *how* as well as knowing *what* – on learning how to learn' (DfEE/QCA, 2000). It places less emphasis on the content of geography and more on the process of enquiry and problem-solving in order for children to develop their understanding of the world by thinking about their thinking and learning, the process of metacognition. Leat (1998) has developed a variety of activities to assist children to think critically about their understanding of the world and how they come to hold views on the spatial processes taking place across it. Distance is also an important concept in developing geographical understanding.

> Distance has two geographic meanings: distance in the lateral sense of the space separating the objects in the mirror in the plane in which they exist, and distance in the vertical sense of the observer's distance from that plane. (Haggett, 1990)

This is an important distinction. Pupils need to understand the effects of distance from a geographical perspective: how long does it take to travel from A to B using different types of transport? What is the best route to take to their field-work destination? But Haggett's second definition is increasingly important with developments in information technology. They allow us to see and read about places, people and events which we never experience at first hand. They may be taking place in the next city or on the other side of the world, but the effect is the same in that it requires us to develop a range of critical skills to assess the accuracy, reliability and validity of the information we are using for geograph-ical enquiry. Thrift (1995) suggests that the huge quantity of global information is resulting in a representation of a complicated world that is 'so complexly inter-connected that some have become to doubt its very legibility'. However, we still need to introduce children to the concept of globalisation as it is a rapidly expanding process. It also has relevant links with developments in information technology: the web enables children to access information and communicate with people around the world. We are only just beginning to consider the effects this may have on our understanding of global events:

> … the Net is not a pipe (nor for that matter, a fire hose) from which children drink, but a beanstalk up which they can climb, like Jack of the fairy tale, into other worlds. (Naughton, 1999)

A central area of understanding in primary geography is that of environmen-tal change and sustainable development.

> In many cultures around the world it is a key social principal the 'the earth is loaned by children to their parents for safe keeping'. This sense of envi-ronmental stewardship lies at the heart of geographical education. (Catling, 1998)

It draws together many of the concepts already discussed such as cause and effect, patterns and processes, along with issues about decision making and thinking. It also enables children to develop their understanding of values and beliefs around the world, as well as starting to develop their own views, hopes and concerns for the world. It provides an excellent opportunity for them to become actively involved in their environment, helping them to begin to under-stand the interaction between people and the physical world which is central to effective geographical understanding.

What Do Legislation and Non-Statutory Documentation Require for Understanding?

In this section I will critically examine two official documents to assess the extent to which they address the need for geographical understanding in primary education: the National Curriculum Order for Geography and the QCA/DfEE Key Stage 1 & 2 Schemes of work for geography, including the teacher's guide update.

> Despite the growing rhetoric about globalisation and citizenship, geography is accorded a relatively low priority in current curriculum policies. (Rawling, 2000)

In her article Rawling provides a detailed analysis of school curriculum requirements and the status of geography. She concludes that the geography education community needs to identify 'new trends and approaches in geography and reshaping them in a dynamic way' and also 'build big ideas for the future'. We will now assess the extent to which legislation requires teachers to build geographical understanding into the primary curriculum perhaps as a means of creating a dynamic pedagogy.

A. The National Curriculum order for geography

The common structure and design for all subjects uses the phrase 'knowledge, skills and understanding' in all national curriculum programmes of study. In the geography order the word understanding first appears in the section headed 'The importance of geography'. It suggests that an understanding of maps is required and that geography is 'a focus within the curriculum for understanding and resolving issues about the environment and sustainable development' (p. 14). Taken as a whole, many professional geographers would support the views expressed. However, it raises the issue of the extent to which non-specialist teachers fully understand the significance of the statements made in the paragraph and the relationships between them. It's a useful statement but requires further elaboration.

The programme of study for Key Stage 1 requires pupils to develop 'knowledge and understanding of places, patterns and processes and environmental change and sustainable development' (p. 16). However, it does not use the word understanding in the section headed geographical enquiry and skills. It appears to take these for granted, suggesting perhaps they are there to support the other sections. Teachers perhaps need further support here to ensure they build in some elements of understanding into the use of skills and the enquiry process: for example to give pupils the opportunity to select appropriate ways of observing and recording. In this way they may increase their understanding of the suitability of various enquiry methods.

The sections headed 'Knowledge and understanding of places', 'Knowledge and understanding of patterns and processes' and 'Knowledge and understanding of environmental change and sustainable development' are interesting. While they use the word 'understanding' in the headings, the body of the texts repeat the words identify, recognise and make observations. The examples concentrate on the more factual aspects of geography such as knowing 'whether they are on a river'. There is very little support for teachers as to what the under-standing aspects of each section might consist of, especially as they are laying down important foundations for an active interest in the world at this key stage. While pupils at Key stage 1 may not have developed some of the mental and linguistic skills needed to demonstrate high levels of understanding, there may be a case for suggesting that teachers, many of whom are non-specialists in geography, need further guidance on the nature of geographical understanding.

The same headings are used in the Key Stage 2 geography orders. However, an analysis of the vocabulary within each section is a little more encouraging in that it provides more opportunities for teachers to plan work which specifically promotes the development of geographical understanding. 'Explain', 'analyse evidence and draw conclusions', 'decision-making skills', 'explain why', 'explain patterns' and 'identify opportunities' are some of the phrases used. The need to develop geographical understanding is much more clearly expressed. As they currently exist, the purpose of the orders is not to provide teachers with detailed subject knowledge and awareness of the meaning of geographical understanding. We need to examine where they may be building up a picture of this from within official documents. Turning to the attainment target for geography on page 43, a more thorough set of ideas is presented as to what may constitute geographical understanding as pupils progress through the levels. Some appropriate examples are provided to demonstrate progress and continuity through the levels. Grimwade argues that:

> Geography is one of the curriculum areas which has integral links to elements of citizenship education delivered in schools. (Grimwade *et al.,* 2000)

Further evidence for the inclusion of the nature of geographical understanding within official documents can be found within the section headed 'Framework for personal, social and health education and citizenship at Key Stages 1 & 2'. At Key Stage 1 it includes ideas such as encouraging children to actively take some responsibility for their environment and to begin to understand the similarities and differences between various groups of people both nearby and further afield. At Key Stage 2 some interesting examples are given which could provide very effective links with geographical understanding. For instance, the guidelines suggest that pupils should be taught:

> ... resources can be allocated in different ways and that these economic choices affect individuals, communities and the sustainability of the environment. (DfEE/QCA, 1999)

and,

> ... to think about the lives of people living in other places and times, and people with different values and customs. (DfEE/QCA, 1999)

These examples echo some of the ideas about geographical understanding discussed in part 1 of this article. The key appears to be the need for teachers to read these documents carefully and to find opportunities to plan interesting activities which will support both effective geographical understanding, the delivery of the statutory orders and the inclusion of ideas presented within these non-statutory guidelines.

The National Curriculum also contains a statement of values. It is interesting to analyse this within the context of geographical understanding, particularly the section headed 'The environment'. It includes, for example, statements suggesting pupils should 'understand the place of human beings within nature' and 'preserve balance and diversity in nature wherever possible'. The seven bullet points all contain strong connections with the ideas discussed in the first section. Again, it appears that there are strong links between various parts of this document which teachers need the confidence to take and use in order to develop effective plans for developing geographical understanding.

B. A scheme of work for Key Stages 1 and 2: Geography

Although the scheme is an optional exemplar it is being used to varying degrees in many primary schools. In the section headed 'Aims and purposes' of geography the word understanding itself is not used, but stimulate, foster, help and enhance are, suggesting a pedagogy based on motivating pupils to see geography as an interesting and lively part of the curriculum.

It becomes even more interesting on page 20 where ideas on evaluating pupils geographical learning are developed. The section headed 'Evaluating the extent to which a scheme of work encourages progression in children's learning' contains eight bullet points explaining how pupils' geographical understanding can progress. It would be most helpful for Key Stage 1 teachers to read this alongside the Key Stage 1 orders in order to see more precisely why their work lays such important foundations for developing geographical understanding. Non-specialist teachers may need further guidance in translating the quite complex geographical concepts contained within this section. However, it is one of the rare examples of writing in these documents which approaches many of the key concepts in geographical understanding and as such could be helpful for all primary teachers to examine in more depth.

The geography teacher's guide update includes a section headed 'Thinking skills'. It states that:

> By using thinking skills children can focus on knowing *how* as well as knowing *what* – on learning how to learn'. (DfEE/QCA, 2000)

This is a clear signal for teachers to move beyond the knowledge aspects of geography and enter the more dynamic arena in which they can study the world as a constantly changing and evolving experience in which both patterns and unique events are constantly occurring.

It includes creative thinking skills and suggests that children should 'apply imagination and to look for alternative innovative outcomes' (DfEE/QCA, 2000): certainly something that links with an understanding of geographical futures and areas of local and global concern. However, so much of what primary teachers have been required to do in the last few years has been highly prescriptive. While Rawling suggests that 'creative curriculum development from the minimal content requirements' (2000: 217) is now a real possibility, to what extent do primary teachers have either the confidence, the time or the levels of subject understanding to enable this to happen, when so much is still expected of them in other aspects of their work?

How Can Teachers Support Children in their Development of that Understanding?

This question needs to be seen in the context of recent developments in primary schools. Since 1998, schools were not required to follow the programmes of study for geography but still had a legal requirement to ensure their curriculum was broad and balanced. In practice, this resulted in some schools marginalising geography and some other foundation subjects, while in others a full programme of work was maintained. In September 2000 geography once again became statutory. However, Literacy and Numeracy continues to demand large sections of the school day. School timetables have become increasingly fixed. Heads, governors and parents do not always understand the value of foundation subjects when there are pressures to meet targets and raise the profile and results of the school. The new inspection regime is changing the pressure on foundation subject during the inspection. Perhaps then, one crucial task for schools in the near future is to ensure that geography receives the time, location and resources needed to help children develop their geographical understanding. If these are limited it is very easy for teachers to resort to activities in geography sessions which focus on knowledge rather than understanding. Teachers need to assess whether quality geographical experiences are best achieved through regular lesson throughout the term, or whether, as some schools are finding, more effective results are achieved where intensive blocks of time are allocated to foundation subjects. Within all these constraints, teachers need to be aware of a number of crucial building blocks which will support them in developing pupils' geographical understanding.

- **Enquiry**
  This is central to developing understanding and critical thinking about the world. Pupils need to actively engage in this process as often as possible. Teachers need to re-establish their own professional confidence in being able to integrate geographical work with other subjects, especially in the core areas, to create more time for quality investigations.

- **Pupils' own experiences**
  Teachers have excellent resources available within their own pupils and the community surrounding the school. Many schools already capitalise on these, creating effective experiences both in geography and citizenship education (*Primary Geographer*, January 2000).

- **Fieldwork**
  Much effective understanding can be developed easily and cheaply in the school locality. First-hand experiences, real issues and local resources all help pupils understand the relevance of geography.

- **ICT**
  Information technology enables children to access geographical data, record, analyse and present their findings. Data loggers can be used in their

locality while the net can be accessed to communicate with people around the world.

- **Human beings and their interaction with the environment**
  Teachers need support in planning learning experiences which help pupils begin to understand the relationship between the human and natural world: rivers cannot be studied merely as physical processes.

- **Patterns and processes**
  Children need carefully planned opportunities in which they can experience a range of patterns and processes taking place in the world.

- **Causes, effects and inter-relationships**
  Geographers study these in almost all they do therefore teachers need to plan learning experiences which will help pupils understand the importance of these concepts in spatial activity.

- **A sense of scale**
  Children's geographical understanding will be developed if they can experience issues and events at a range of scales: litter in school, refuse management in their town, to what happens to nuclear waste around the world?

- **Environmental issues and sustainable development**
  These provide real world opportunities to develop an understanding of cause and effect and aspects of citizenship at a range of scales.

- **A sense of time, space and change**
  At a very local scale, how has their room at home changed during the last year? Why has this happened? What would they like to stay the same and what would they like to change? How is it similar and different to their best friend's room down the street?

Today's pupils are tomorrow's global citizens who will need a highly developed sense of geographical understanding as technology will link them more and more to events, patterns and processes around the world. Will they sink under the illegibility described by Thrift (1995) or will they experience what Haggett explains in this way:

> To see where something fits in the spatial order of the great global jigsaw is a supreme if rare reward. (Haggett, 1990)

This enables children, like Alice, to see just that little bit further.

Correspondence

Any correspondence should be directed to Mr John Halocha, Senior Lecturer in Primary education, Bishop Grossteste College, Lincoln LN1 3DY, UK (j.w.halocha@bgc.ac.uk).

References

Carroll, L. (1872) *Through the Looking Glass and What Alice Found There.*
Catling, S. (1998) Geography in the National Curriculum and beyond. In R. Carter (ed.) *Handbook of Primary Geography*. Sheffield: Geographical Association.
DfEE/QCA (1998) *Geography: A Scheme of Work for Key Stages 1 and 2*. London: DfEE/QCA.
DfEE/QCA (1999) *Geography: The National Curriculum for England*. London: DfEE/QCA.
DfEE/QCA (2000) *Geography. Teacher's Guide Update*. London: QCA.

Grimwade, K., Jackson, E., Reid, A. and Smith, M. (2000) *Geography and the New Agenda: Citizenship, PSHE and Sustainable Development in the Primary School*. Sheffield: Geographical Association.

Haggett, P. (1990) *The Geographer's Art*. Oxford: Basil Blackwell.

Hart, P. and Nolan, K. (1999) A critical analysis of research in environmental education. *Studies in Science Education* 34.

Hicks, D. (1994) *Educating for the Future: A Practical Classroom Guide*. London: World Wide Fund for Nature.

Hillman, M. (1993) *Children, Transport and the Quality of Life*. London: Policy Studies Institute.

Jameson, F. (1991) *Postmodernism*. London: Verso.

Johnson, R.J., Taylor, P.J. and Watts, M.J. (eds) (1995) *Geographies of Global Change: Remapping the World in the Late Twentieth Century*. Oxford: Blackwell.

Leat, D. (ed.) (1998) *Thinking Through Geography*. Cambridge: Chris Kington Publishing.

Naughton, J. (1999) *A Brief History of the Future: The Origins of the Internet*. London: Weidenfeld and Nicolson.

Primary Geographer (2000) Number 4, January 2000. Sheffield: Geographical Association.

Rawling, E. (2000) Ideology, politics and curriculum change: Reflections on school Geography 2000. *Geography* 83 (3), 209–220.

Smeaton, M. (1998) Questioning geography. In R. Carter (ed.) *Handbook of Primary Geography*. Sheffield: Geographical Association.

Thrift, N. (1995) A hyperactive world. In R.J. Johnson, P.J. Taylor and M.J. Watts (eds) *Geographies of Global Change: Remapping the World in the Late Twentieth Century*. Oxford: Blackwell.

Encouraging Historical Understanding in the Primary Classroom

Lynn D. Newton
University of Durham, School of Education, Leazes Road, Durham DH1 1TA, UK

In this paper, what counts as understanding in history is considered. Some strategies that have been shown by research to be effective in supporting the construction of historical understanding are discussed and the implications for teachers' practices are identified.

Introduction

History is a record of the events of human affairs. The problem in making this record is that the events are past and gone and have to be reconstructed from what remains. Although a historical event is unique, events do not occur in isolation and evidence is likely to be incomplete and uncertain. Inevitably, several plausible accounts of it are often possible. As mental constructions, these accounts are our understandings of the event. These understandings cannot, of course, be put to the test because a historical event can never be run again (nor would it be ethical to do so, even given the possibility). Instead, the understanding judged to be the most plausible tends to gain pre-eminence pending further revision and reconstruction (Becher, 1994; Emmet, 1985; Humphreys, 1989).

A reconstruction that orders the occurrences in an event and presents them in a temporal sequence could be said to be an understanding. This kind of under-standing could enable a step-by-step description of the event. Often, a historian attempts to do more and explain why the event occurred, telling a story that depicts why the event unfolded as it did. The reasons in this story (the 'becauses') generally refer to human behaviours in relation to the context. This is often described as establishing causal relationships (Evans, 1997) but the word 'cause' has deterministic connotations that some historians prefer to avoid. Oakeshott (1983) preferred 'antecedent condition' to 'cause' and Haydn *et al.* (1997) prefer 'consequence' to 'effect'.

An understanding of a historical event, therefore, is the construction of an ordered mental representation of matters and occurrences considered to comprise or bear upon the event. It usually includes reasons why that sequence took the direction it did. Often, the construction is uncertain so this understanding is one of several that may be plausible (Newton, 2000).

Young Children Understanding History

Given the purpose of history as a record of human events, the aim is to help children understand such events. While children may be mentally capable of giving reasons for events, what counts in history (or any other subject, for that matter) has to be learned. For instance, the explanation of, 'Why did the Span-iards fail to invade England in …?' would produce different answers in history, science, geography, and design and technology. Even 10-year-olds do not

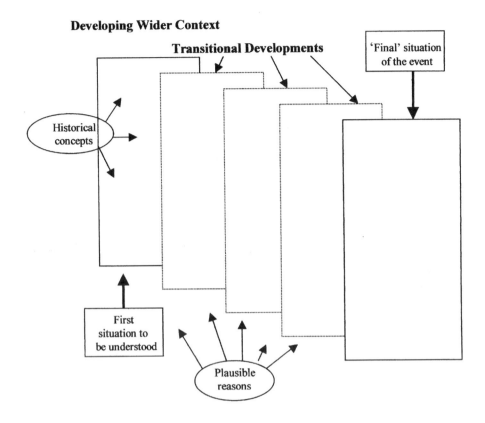

Figure 1 Understanding an historical event – a learning pathway

always know what counts in different subjects when depending on their own resources. The failure of the invasion, for instance, might be ascribed entirely to the behaviour of material objects.

In a research project in which he attempted to map children's ideas about historical accounts, Peter Lee (1998) gave older primary pupils (7–8 years and 10–11 years) and younger secondary pupils (11–12 years and 13–14 years) two pictorially supported stories of a historical event. The two accounts were presented running side by side down an A4 sheet of paper and the pupils were asked questions about the differences. The children were also asked to explain how it was possible to obtain two different views about 'the same bit of history'. The event related to the Romans in Britain. From analysis of the responses of 320 pupils, Lee found a clear progression in pupils' ideas about historical accounts, reflecting a progression in concepts of evidence and perspectives:

(1)   *The past is given* ... stories 'about the same thing' are the same story.
(2)   *The past is inaccessible* ... we can never know because we were not there. Nothing can be known – differences in accounts result from lack of direct access.

(3) *The past is determining stories* ... stories are fixed by the information available; differences arise from lack of information and mistakes.

(4) *The past is reported in a more or less biased way* ... differences in accounts are a result in distorted reporting, reflecting a contribution by the writer; the problem is more than just lack of information.

(5) *The past is selected and organised from a particular viewpoint* ... stories are not copies of the past; the differences are a result of selection, reflecting the position and viewpoint of the writer.

(6) *The past is (re-)constructed in answer to questions in accordance with criteria* ... recognition that it is the nature of the accounts that differ, with a shift of focus from the author's perspective and choice to the nature of the accounts themselves.

(After Lee, 1998: 34)

It seems from the evidence that the younger (7–8 year old) pupils were more 'certain' about the historical accounts. They tended to view the accounts as the same, differing only in the way they were told. Differences were seen as arising from differences between the narrators and the vocabulary they used, not the ideas being described. They were more likely to attribute differences to lack of knowledge on the part of the narrator.

Primary age pupils learn what counts from repeated exposure to it and through the teacher's guidance (Newton & Newton, 1999). Given that they have this guidance, there are still requisites that facilitate or enable a particular historical understanding. These elements of knowledge are the building blocks of an understanding of an event. For instance, understanding an event might call for a grasp of:

- objects and their function (e.g. a castle, the steam engine, flint tools);
- concepts (e.g. ruler, king, law and power);
- structures (e.g. the feudal system, crop rotation, monastic life);
- physical constraints (e.g. housing, clothing, food, health, transport, war);
- social mores and tendencies in behaviours (e.g. what people valued and aspired to, motives, desires, ambitions, strengths and weaknesses);
- other occurrences and events that lead up to or otherwise bear upon the one to be understood (e.g. job shortages, famine, arrival of the railway age);
- how things hang together chronologically (e.g. sequences and changes over time).

Suppose, for instance, that children were faced with constructing an understanding of Guy Fawkes' attempt to blow up the Houses of Parliament. They would need to know the objects involved (such as, gunpowder, barrel, fuse, Houses of Parliament) thus allowing a descriptive understanding of the situation. It might help to know that there were no aircraft in those days (explaining why there was not an air-strike or an attempt to escape by helicopter). It could help to know the function of the Houses of Parliament (providing a reason for the choice of site). A grasp of what people feel, value and desire would support the understanding (strength of feeling motivating action in spite of great personal risk), as it would the response to the attempt. Here is a 6-year-old's account of the event, corrected only for spelling:

> There was this king. There was a man who wanted to blow up. There was a plot. They got barrels of gunpowder. They went under the Houses of Parliament. They let a man Guy Fawkes hide in between it. He didn't want them to do it. His brother worked in the Houses of Parliament. A man grabbed a horse. He told the police. Some got caught by getting killed. Some didn't. They got caught alive. Then they got killed. They lived happily ever after.

This young child has grasped elements of the story. More than that, this is not just a blow by blow account of the event. The child has constructed an understanding that incorporates a reason (indicating that Guy Fawkes was concerned about his brother's safety so did not want the attempt to be made). In that sense, this is an explanatory understanding. It has a long way to go to be like that of a historian but it has obvious potential for further development. For instance, why did they want to blow up the Houses of Parliament? It is probable that this child understood more than she said in her account but it does remind us that the same event can be understood in different ways, at various levels and to different degrees. It would be reasonable for us to expect more from, say, a 10-year old.

A fundamental concept in history is the idea of change over time. For primary age children, the time scale from one birthday to the next is a long time. The concept of a timescale spanning decades, centuries or millennia can be quite challenging. Research by Barton and Levstik (1996) indicates that young children can, for instance, distinguish pictures of places and people according to the historical period but they have difficulty with the significance of dates, historical periods and epochs. Most third graders (8–9 year olds) can get to grips with historical dates and sequence them, but it takes another two or three years before the concept of a time line is fully appreciated.

Helping Young Children Understand History

How do we go about preparing children to understand historical events and supporting the processes involved? To return to the model provided in Figure 1, it is clear that there are several important stages, at any or all of which support can be provided.

First, there are the requisites. One of the problems with history is there do not appear to be any real 'beginnings'. How do we create a starting point for the historical situation or event? The teacher needs to identify a starting point and be clear about the flow of 'happenings' and why things took the course they did. This will lead to planning with clear targets in mind and explicit types of understanding to be developed as the history topic unfolds.

The next step would be to find out what ideas and experiences the children are bringing to the situation. Related concepts and ideas, prior experiences with a material bearing on the new events and key vocabulary can all be recalled and rehearsed. This provides a broader context into which the new events can be embedded. Some strategies might include:

- holding a class brainstorming session;
- concept mapping or concept cartoon activities about the situation or event;
- using question–answer games to identify what the children already know;

- organising the children to create big books or floor books about their current ideas;

Obviously, the ages and abilities of the children would determine the choice of strategy.

In this initial state, supporting the grasp of historical concepts and terms is very important. Greenwood (1988) has pointed out that learning a list of words is a decontextualised task and risks acquired meanings being vague. Analogies can be used to develop young children's vocabulary in history as in other subjects areas (Newton, 2000). For a young child, a ruler is a piece of wood or plastic with a straight edge used for measuring. A ruler of a country is an abstract concept, but to liken a ruler to a captain of a ship who gives the orders and is obeyed might make it more meaningful.

Bridging analogies can aid the mental shift from the known to the unknown. To explain the abstract concept of democracy in Ancient Greece a teacher could use the concrete concept of class discussions, turn taking, voting, and so on. Such analogies can also be used to link chronology to a time line. Helping children to create their own personal time line or family time line can precede the longer scale historical time line. A visual creation (a border around the classroom) can help locate their immediate position in the greater scheme of things. Sutton (1996) argues persuasively that pupils often need to adopt another perspective in order to understand it in the way a specialist might. He suggests that perspectives stem from the language, metaphors and analogies of the subject and non-experts need to learn these in order to change perspectives.

The next stage involves the process of constructing an understanding of events – the story with reasons. How do we do this? The aim is to introduce and explore the new situation or event so that descriptive or situational understanding can be constructed. The key characters are introduced, their motives and feeling explored, the relevant events going on around them described, and the sequence of those events given. This all provides the immediate context for the new understanding and justifies why the starting point is the way it is. Some strategies to support this stage might include:

- stories and poems with an historical focus;
- pictures and video/film archive materials;
- dramatic re-enactments of historical events;
- historical artefacts;
- visits to places of historical interest.

In all cases, the important role of language and discussion is fundamental. Atmosphere created about the historical event acts as a great motivator to the learning process. Yekovich *et al.* (1991) identify this initial situation as crucial in the construction of understanding. The relationships that are to be inferred if events are to be understood must be known or capable of construction. The learner must be able to discriminate between the relevant and the irrelevant information. Finally the children must recognise the need to do something with that information and be willing to do so. Links and connections to prior experiences will be made and, perhaps, visits and stories will help to consolidate this state.

As the story unfolds and the event flows the children will revisit and update their present understandings in the light of the new experiences and ideas to give new mental states. These transitional states are all important in developing and consolidating the historical understandings and encouraging historical empathy. They bridge gaps and, as such, must be clear and explicit enough to support the changing understandings. Beck *et al.* (1991) illustrated the improvement in understanding of 10-year-olds that resulted from taking into account prerequisites, gap bridging and explaining. Working on historical text, they list a number of reasons why a learner may fail to make connections amongst the elements of information:

- inadequate background knowledge;
- the use of references that are ambiguous, distant or indirect;
- the lack of information to activate an appropriate context;
- the lack of clear connections between events;
- the inclusion of irrelevant events and ideas; and,
- a high density of concepts.

Beck *et al.* tested their ideas by revising a history text for 10–year-olds. They clarified, elaborated, provided missing information and made connections explicit in the text. The effect was to make the text much longer but the gain in meaning was significant.

The final stage involves checking that the children have grasped the key ideas and can give plausible reasons for outcomes. The important point here is to check that the children know *why* these are plausible. Often, we present historical events as predigested stories. Narrative, of course, is a form well known to children and readily grasped by them. Teachers can, and often do, use this to advantage. This approach can risk concealing the possibility that other plausible understandings are feasible. Attempts to overcome this are generally based on having the children be 'history detectives' for some local event and drawing on primary sources, such as newspapers and recollections of grandparents. In the early 1980s, the Domesday Project was a national event, involving schools and various community groups in surveying their local communities to collect local, historical, social, geographical and other relevant information to be entered on an interactive video disk (IVD). Many primary schools took part, being allocated a grid reference area to survey. All data were collected centrally and the IVD was created which then became accessible to anyone with the appropriate technology to use it (mainly schools and similar institutions). The first hand, practical experiences helped children to recall relevant prior knowledge and experiences and relate these to the new experiences in the local context.

Another strategy which serves a similar purpose in supporting understanding is to visit a site of historical interest, especially if role play can be involved so that the children can experience the historical event. Bede's World in Jarrow is such a site. The children can dress as monks, experience the daily routine of the monastery, carry out a range of tasks and enjoy a typical monk's meal. At the Beamish Museum, they can step back into Victorian times and experience what life was like. Home and school, transport and shopping, a trip to the dentist or working down a mine, all can be shown to them. Trying to recreate the story of someone else's life can be done in the classroom if a visit is not possible. The children can become historical detectives to recreate the person who owns the 'found' suitcase or the family who threw out the bag of rubbish. Such concrete experiences help the children move through the various transitional stages identified in Figure 1 as they work towards the final situation to be understood.

All of these activities, one way or another, lead to constructing explanations – explanatory understanding – of why things are they way they are or events took the course they did. This is the final state of understanding we want the children to achieve but, of course, is only the starting point for further understanding.

Correspondence

Any correspondence should be directed to Dr Lynn Newton, University of Durham, School of Education, Leazes Road. Durham DH1 1TA (l.d.newton@durham.ac.uk).

References

Barton, K.C. and Levstik, L.S. (1996) Back when God was around and everything. *American Educational Research Journal* 33, 36–49.

Becher, T. (1994) The significance of disciplinary differences. *Studies in Higher Education.* 19, 151–61.

Beck, I.L., McKeown, M.G., Sinatra, G.M. and Loxterman, J.A. (1991) Revising social studies text from a text processing perspective: Evidence of Improved comprehensibility. *Reading Research Quarterly* 26, 251–276.

Emmet, D. (1985) *The Effectiveness of Causes.* Albany: State University of New York Press.

Evans, R.J. (1997) *In Defence of History.* London: Granta.

Greenwood, S.C. (1988) How to use analogy instruction to reinforce vocabulary. *Middle School Journal* 19, 11–13.

Haydn, T., Arthur, J. and Hunt, M. (1997) *Learning to Teach History in the Secondary School.* London: Routledge.

Humphreys, P. (1989) *The Chances of Explanation.* Princeton, NJ: Princeton University Press.

Lee, P. (1998) A lot of guess work goes on. Children's understanding of historical accounts. *Teaching History* 92, 29–36.

Newton, D.P. (2000) *Teaching for Understanding.* London: Routledge Falmer.

Newton, D.P. and Newton, L.D. (1999) Knowing what counts as understanding in different disciplines: Some ten-year-olds conceptions. *Educational Studies* 25, 35–54.

Oakeshott, M. (1983) *On History.* Oxford: Blackwell.

Sutton, C. (1996) The scientific model as a form of speech. In G. Welford, J. Osborne and P. Scott (eds) *Research in Science Education in Europe.* London: Falmer Press.

Yekovich, F.R., Thompson, M.A. and Walker, C.H. (1991) Generation and verification of inferences by experts and trained nonexperts. *American Educational Research Journal* 28, 189–209.

Expression in the Visual Arts

Peter Millward and Anthony Parton
University of Durham, School of Education, Leazes Road, Durham, DH1 1TA, UK

Behind all the valuable guidance offered in the *National Curriculum for Art and Design* booklet (QCA/DfEE, 1999) and through the suggestions in the *Art & Design Scheme of Work* (QCA/DfEE, 2000), lies a level of thinking for teachers which may not be readily apparent. This level of thinking might be described by the question: What is it like to work as an artist, an art critic or a reader of art works? The answer might be found only in the 'experience' of working as an artist, an art critic or a reader of art works. Whilst this kind of experience is implicit in much of the National Curriculum documentation, we believe it can easily get lost. The experience required can be gained only by exploring art mediums, making and reading art and by working in the company of people who know about art. Experience is all, and whilst the National Curriculum documents provide plenty of opportunities and suggestions for giving children experience of working with a range of art materials, this experience must be shaped if the participants are to develop artistic understanding and appreciation. This paper focuses upon how the construction of such an understanding can be supported in the primary phase of education.

Introduction

We believe that behind all of the children's work in the expressive visual arts must lie a context in which people can work meaningfully as artists, as art critics and as 'readers' of art. The children should know what it feels like to read a work of art, to work as an artist and to talk about their art with other artists. The provision of contexts for making, reading, exploring and commenting upon art forms might be the prime achievement of the visual arts teacher trying to develop the expressive arts in the classroom. An 'atmosphere of art' pervades the Art and Design documents, but the prescriptive quality in the National Curriculum might mean that it is lost in practice. It is our purpose in this article to draw attention to some of the necessary features of creating contexts in which children can flourish as artists. The key to this is 'expression in the arts'. If expression is not part of the classroom experience, the teacher and the children will not be working as artists; and they may find it quite hard to be expressive whilst attending to the requirements of the National Curriculum documents. To be able to express themselves in the visual arts children must have some measure of control over the process and that means expressing themselves purposefully and with intention. The artist is the author of his or her work, and we must remember this if we are to help children to express themselves artistically.

For the purpose of this article, we are going to focus on painting in the visual arts and, as examples, we will discuss Kandinsky's well known series of *Compositions* from 1912 to 1914, and a painting by a child aged 9 years which we refer to as *Aiden's Picture* of 2000 (Figure 1). Kandinsky's paintings employ abstraction. They exemplify the artist's attempt to effect a spiritual transformation in the viewer by 'liberating' the expressive potential of colour and line through the process of abstraction. For Kandinsky, abstracted colour and line could directly affect the emotions and soul of the spectator and could be 'orchestrated', like music, to achieve specific ends. Imagery, however, was still germane to his work

Figure 1 Aiden's picture

and, although abstracted or 'veiled' as he put it, it is none the less present. In his *Compositions* we can trace vestiges of apocalyptic images from the book of *Revelation* (angels with trumpets, images of Leviathan and storms at sea, etc.). This hidden imagery was designed to work hand-in-hand with the expressive power of colour and line to achieve Kandinsky's aim of creating a spiritual change in the viewer. Aiden's *Picture* was painted having seen Kandinsky's work and having considered its 'veiled' subject matter. It represents a response not only to the shapes and colours that Kandinsky uses but also to the 'veiled' imagery of tempestuous storms in Kandinsky's paintings. We will look closer at Aiden's work later in the article.

Expression in paintings such as these is conventionally negotiated through content and form. We may call 'content' the subject matter of the art work whilst the 'form' is the style or technique the artist has adopted to express the content. So, a child artist might use the formal aspects of tone and colour to express opposing qualities of calm and stormy weather and invite the reader, through incongruity in composition (setting night and day together, for example, in one painting), to wonder about some of the deep conflicts in experience which is the content of the painting. Aiden's *Picture* supports complex analysis and critical commentary and suggests that the child is engaged in the same activity as an adult artist such as Kandinsky. In his *Compositions* Kandinsky uses texture, brushwork, colour, line, pictorial space and composition to express the nature of conflict on a cosmic scale. Aidan might have reduced the conflict to more manageable horizons as he produces clear accounts of night and day in a readily accessible landscape, but the essential relationships between form and content are still apparent and illuminating.

Expression in the visual arts implies an artist with an intention to communicate through art and a reader with an interest in responding to a work of art. To paint expressively, the artist must engage with the medium. This means s/he must draw upon technical skills in painting, make decisions about the medium (choice of colour, paper and brush, for example), develop ways of working the medium (through, say, line, shape and texture) and be constantly sensitive to the developing composition. The artist's work presupposes an audience and is defined, at least in part, by the audience. There is a reflexive relationship here: the artist's engagement with the medium, the making of the art work, and the reading of the art work, take place in a shared cultural context. It is this context that needs to be developed by the art teacher and the children with whom s/he is working. It is a context defined by artistic expression.

The audience for children's artistic expression is dominated by adults and, primarily, by teachers and parents. Adults have views about art, and adult audiences have expectations about art and about children's art. Children who thrive in school are sensitive to adults' expectations and keep them in mind as they express their views artistically. Children who work for teachers, work for a very powerful and influential audience, and the visual arts teacher is not a disinterested reader, but a reader with a professional concern to make judgements about the child and about the child's work. The teacher is concerned to judge the child as a pupil as well as an artist. The teacher knows too that his or her performance as a teacher of visual arts will be judged by the 'quality' of the child's art work. These levels of concern in the audience are bound to affect children's expression in the visual arts and it is easy for children to 'paint for teacher'. However, the situation in school is still more complicated for this powerful audience is likely to define a significant part of the child's intention and may control the medium and the child's engagement with the medium. When a teacher asks a child to 'paint some mountains by the sea', s/he puts real constraints on the child's choice and use of form, and describes content in quite specific terms. It is not hard to imagine the kind of picture the teacher might want, and most children will rise to the occasion, but their paintings may not have the same depth and complexity as Aiden's *Picture*, which might be referred to as 'mountains by the sea'.

We are inclined to think of expression in the arts as an opportunity for self-expression; but self-expression is mightily constrained. It is constrained not simply by the imagination of the child and by his or her technical ability, but also by the medium, by the audience and by the specific social and cultural contexts in which it is developed. These constraints are shared by all artists, but the extra authority given to the teacher in the classroom, supported by the requirements of the National Curriculum is likely to describe the context and make it difficult for the child to express him or herself artistically. Of course, we cannot take the child/artist out of the teaching context, but the teacher must be aware that when s/he describes what counts as successful expression (in terms of what the child should express, how the child should express it and the medium through which it should be expressed) and when s/he goes on to determine how successful the child has been, s/he is likely to make it very difficult for the child to work as an artist. The teacher's role is certain to be problematic. It is a role that cannot be taken for granted and teachers have to learn to respond as readers of art if they are to help children develop intentions that can be realised through art. The teacher needs to think carefully about the pressures s/he puts upon the child and needs to seek for ways in which the child can be helped to work more like an artist.

At every stage, artistic expression involves a level of exploration. The artist is exploring the world (the world of art and the world of everyday life, and the relationship between the two), exploring the medium and exploring his or her technique. It is through this exploration that the child artist expresses more than s/he meant to express and discovers something of what s/he has expressed. Aiden may look at his finished painting and can say a bit more about his experience of life as it is represented in the conflict between night and day, calm and stormy weather, earth and water and mountains and plains. He will also know a little more about the way in which his experience may be expressed in formal terms and there may be a realisation that this view can only be constructed through art. If this does not happen then herein lies the opportunity for the teacher to teach, and the teacher will do so by reading the child artist's work. The reader 'reading' art is bound to explore the painting, the making of the painting and the experience of life and art associated with the painting. When we look at Aiden's picture we talk about our response in terms of the artist's work, his use of paint, the composition of his painting and the way in which it connects with our experience of conflict in art and in everyday life. Expression in the visual arts does not mean we know what we want to show or that we know all that we have shown. Expression in the visual arts involves interpretation and a shared exploration. It involves talking about the child's intention in the light of his or her knowledge and ability, the medium worked and the audience to which the expressive intentions are directed. It means developing, and helping to make explicit, the context within which the child artist paints.

In order to understand expression in the arts it is necessary for children to think about art, to read art and to make art.

Children Thinking About Art

If children are to take control of their art then teachers must encourage them to think about art. The National Curriculum offers children and teachers plenty of opportunity to do this. At Key Stage 1 they are encouraged to wonder about artists and how they think and feel about paintings.[1] At Key Stage 2 they are expected to 'increase their critical awareness of the roles and purposes of art ... by commenting on works and asking questions'.[2] Children need to appreciate that there is a language of visual art that is used to manage and sustain artistic experience. This language has its own vocabulary and descriptors and its own criteria for identifying artistic endeavour and assessing value in art. The language is often shifted towards the expression of affective experience and there are strong moral and aesthetic features. It has an interpretative quality. This language is used to talk about the arts at a universal level as well as in relation to specific art works and processes. On a universal level it is used to compare art works and artists, to generate ideas about the arts, to define periods and movements in the arts and to relate art works to social and cultural contexts. In relation to specific art works, the language of art enables children to: 'explore ideas about starting points for work', 'ask and answer questions about source materials', 'discuss and compare their own work and others' work', 'explain their own views'.[3] They can consider the way in which paintings relate to historical and cultural settings, identify inter-textual relationships, and critically review a painting and their response to the painting.

Children and their teachers have to appreciate that this language of art – in both its universal and specific usage – is not in addition to the practice and appreciation of art. It is an essential feature of art practice and without this linguistic context for art and artistic expression, there would be no art. It is part of the way in which art is defined in our culture and part of the way in which it is described and experienced as a discrete area of knowledge and understanding. Children must be introduced to this language even as they begin to engage in arts based activities because as artists they are required to talk about their work; as readers they must find words to justify and explain their response to a work of art and as critics they must support their judgement by reference to specific features of the work. The linguistic context serves to keep a check on art and keeps us safe from idiosyncratic and emotional outpourings. To engage in art is to talk about art, and artists (and children and teachers doing art) cannot step outside the bounds of their language.

Children Reading Art

Not every child will become an artist and not every child will want to express him or herself through art. We have to accept that, and we have to accept that we cannot make children present experience artistically. However, every child is entitled to experience art and every child is entitled to learn how to read art.

If children are to understand expression in the arts they must gain experience in reading art forms and they must develop this experience in the company of people who understand art and who can talk about art. Reading art is demanding and the kind of understanding a child needs to read art is not easy to grasp and is developed through guided experience. It is not made easier by treating the process as simple.

Children need to appreciate, for example, that a painting is a representation of an artist's experience of life. Kandinsky's *Compositions*, for example, might be opened up at a number of levels from the basic reading of them as an expression of storm and destruction to the more subtle view of the paintings as an expression of Kandinsky's own emotions mediated via the metaphors of form and content. Children have to approach a work of art in the knowledge that it has been made with the intention that others may come to read it and, at some level, share experience. In order to read a painting, the child must understand that the painting represents life and that the painter is not just trying to copy life as closely as possible. It is important for children to appreciate that phrases like 'true to life' or 'life like' do not mean 'the same as life', and that 'true to life' and 'life like' do not mean the same as art. Kandinsky is a good example in this respect since the expressive potential of abstract colour and line could, in his view, express more about his feelings and could move the viewer more powerfully than a straightforward mimetic transcription of a storm. It is the responsibility of the reader to 'connect' the art work with his or her experience of life and to create this relationship, and children need to take account of their lives and account of their experience of art. Children and their teachers have to understand that expression in the arts means focusing on the relationship between art and everyday experience. It also means attending to the form and the content of the art work and to the ways in which they illuminate each other. In this respect Aiden's *Picture* is successful since he carefully chooses threatening triangular shapes to dominate the composition, a grey/green palette of colours and dark tones with which to suggest the onset of a storm. It is interesting that this choice is by no means arbitrary since Aiden himself in writing about his work associates the triangles of the mountain range with 'witches' hats' and 'witches' noses'. The content is seen through the form, but the form is explicable only through the reader's appreciation of the content. Reading art is about reading relationships and children have to read many relationships, for example, those between artist, art work and reader; between form and content; between painting as process and painting as a work of art; between art work and everyday life; between an art work and other works of art, and between art and the language of art. Reading art is a complex and subtle activity, and it depends upon engaging with a range of art works in the company of teachers who know about art and know about the processes of making and reading art. Children learn to read art by talking about art.

But each child reads art in a different way, and each child needs to appreciate that there is not a definitive reading of any art work, but only another interpretation. It is because we read art differently that we talk about art and that we have to talk about art. It is through our talk about art that we develop responses that are not idiosyncratic, and it is through our talk that we learn to explain our reading in the language of art. There is a dialogue that keeps artists and their readers in touch, and children have to learn to take part in the dialogue. Teachers and artists can guide the child's reading, but nobody can tell the child what s/he should read in the painting.

As children develop their experience of reading art and sharing a dialogue, they will come to appreciate that reading art is important. It can change our lives and it can change what we know about life. It affects the way we feel about life, about art and about ourselves. Reading art is closely related to our own sense of identity and we read ourselves through our reading of art. Reading art is rewarding and it leads directly to making art.

Children Making Art

Children have to appreciate that whilst their art connects with their experience of life, it does not have to copy or replicate that experience. The desperate quest for accurate reproductions of the world ('horses don't have legs like that' or 'you can't have night and day at the same time' – Figure 1) is bound to be depressing for children and for their teachers. It seems that children should be released from the empty demands of mimesis. They should be encouraged to feel that their representations reach beyond their everyday experience of life and reach towards an 'inner life', and a life which might only be revealed through art. When children are encouraged to find associations between feelings and colour, they are heading in this direction. They should be helped to appreciate that the link between art and life is an associative link, and that is a link that is endlessly fascinating.

To forge the link, children have to explore life and what it is like to be alive and they have to explore a variety of art mediums. They should look closely at their experience of life and they should experiment with the medium to see how it works and how it can be worked. It is only through knowing about life and knowing about paint and painting, that they can seek for ways to make their pictures express aspects of their experience of life. Learning about life and learning about art are at the heart of artistic expression. If children want to express themselves artistically, they will need to be able to do so in a purposeful way. They will need to be able to reflect upon their lives, and they will need a measure of control over the aspects of their experience they want to explore and present in their art. Equally, they will need a measure of control over the medium they use to explore and present experience artistically. They will need, as well, to be able to control the ways in which they use the medium to produce their art.

This measure of control requires a disciplined approach and this discipline is not simply a matter of managing technique. It is contained in the language and practices of art. Whilst we can provide contexts in which to develop artistic awareness and sensibility, we cannot make a person express him or herself artistically and the discipline of the artist must be managed from within. It is a discipline which is described by the artist's perception of his or her world, the medium through which the artist's view will be presented, and the artist's sensitivity towards his or her audience. The engagement around a work of art is like a dialogue in which the participants express themselves in ways that are sensitive to the interests and perceptions of the artists and readers involved. It is a self-motivated engagement.

Implications for Teachers

In our view the discussion above raises several important implications for teachers seeking to promote expression in the visual arts in the classroom.

The teacher must:

- accept his or her responsibility to know about art.
- be prepared to make art in the company of children and seek to become a working model of an artist.
- provide a context in which children can work as artists
- accept his or her role as an audience for the work that children create and respond as an interested person as well as a teacher.
- be prepared to make his or her response to the children's work explicit
- think carefully about the pressures put on children who art expected to 'paint for teacher'
- realise that artistic activity cannot be separated from its cultural setting. S/he must be open to the complex nexus of influences working upon the child;
- foster a degree of technical ability in relation to the medium but remember that the making of art operates in the broader context of language and practice of art;
- remember that teaching does not end when a child has finished creating an art work but continues in the form of discussion and into the next piece of work so that a coherent tradition is fostered in the child;
- remember that art reflects upon life and that life feeds into art.

Understanding expression in the visual arts means appreciating that people use art forms to represent their experiences of life and that people use art forms to reflect upon their experiences of life. It means appreciating that, as artists or as readers of art we have to engage actively with life and with art forms and that we have to be aware of our engagement. It means a willing engagement with eyes wide open. It means understanding what you are about.

Notes

1. The National Curriculum for Art and Design, Programme of Study, Key Stage 1, p. 16.
2. A Scheme of Work for Key Stages 1 and 2: Art & Design p.4
3. The National Curriculum for Art and Design, Programme of Study, Key Stage 1–2, pp. 16–18.

Correspondence

Any correspondence should be directed to Dr Anthony Parton, University of Durham, School of Education, Leazes Road, Durham DH1 1TA, UK (anthony.parton@durham.ac.uk).

References

QCA/DfEE (1999) *The National Curriculum for Art and Design: Key Stages 1–3.*
QCA/DfEE (2000) *A Scheme of Work for Key Stages 1 and 2: Art & Design.*

Teaching for Understanding: Curriculum Guidance for the Foundation Stage

Eve English
University of Durham, School of Education, Leazes Road, Durham DH1 1TA, UK

This paper briefly considers what research has told us about the development of young children's understanding. It goes on to look at the *Curriculum Guidance for the Foundation Stage* (QCA, 2000) in terms of that research. The paper suggests that the guidance has addressed concerns that early years practitioners might be delivering an inappropriate curriculum in their attempts to reach targets. The published guidance is giving a clear message that an early years curriculum is quite different from that provided for older children and that our knowledge of child development should be the driving force in delivering that curriculum.

Introduction

September 2000 saw the introduction of a foundation stage for children aged three to the end of reception year. To support this foundation stage QCA (Qualifications and Curriculum Authority) has developed accompanying curriculum guidance (*Curriculum Guidance for the Foundation Stage (QCA, 2000)*). For the first time in this country, pre-school and reception year children have been provided with their own curriculum that purports to be relevant to their needs. For teachers of pre-school children a common curriculum is provided regardless of the educational setting. For teachers of reception year children there is now a recognition that all children in that year group need a discrete curriculum and it removes the previous confusion that arose from the requirement that a child should follow the National Curriculum from his/her 5th birthday. The foundation curriculum is designed to help early years practitioners plan towards the *Early Learning Goals* (October, 1999). These replaced the *Desirable Outcomes For Children's Learning* (SCAA, 1996). These Early Learning Goals describe expectations deemed to be achievable for most children by the end of the foundation stage. In this way they are equivalent to the attainment targets of the National Curriculum.

There has been some concern (e.g. Edwards & Knight, 1994) that the curriculum offered to young children has been a diluted version of the National Curriculum and that teachers have been finding it difficult 'to sustain the well-established principles of early childhood education in their practice' (Early Years Curriculum Group, 1998). The *Curriculum Guidance for the Foundation Stage* is providing the opportunity for practitioners to build on their knowledge of child development and provide a curriculum that is more appropriate to the needs of young children.

> Children, aged three, four and five are constantly encountering new experiences and seeking to understand them in order to extend their skills, develop their confidence and build on what they already know. They learn in many different ways. Practitioners have a crucial role in this learning and should draw on a range of teaching and care strategies and knowledge of child development. (QCA, 2000: 6)

This paper will consider the *Curriculum Guidance for the Foundation Stage* in terms of how it addresses the issue of young children's understanding.

What is Understanding in the Early Years?

Newton (2000: 191) described understanding as being about 'getting a handle on things', about being able to make connections between facts and ideas, and being able to see relationships and patterns. He was describing the importance of children's understanding in the context of primary science, but it is equally important in all areas of the curriculum and to all children, whatever their age. Understanding, as opposed to memorisation, is essential if children are to make sense of their world, if they are to learn by connecting new information to what they already know, if they are to remember what they have learned and if they are to solve problems (Newton, 2000: 192).

Teachers' knowledge of children's understanding is informed by different theories of cognitive development. Piagetian theory has been very influential in describing the stages of thinking that children go through and the recognition that children actively construct their own learning through their interactions with the environment. This has led to teaching approaches that recognise the importance of young children being directly involved in their learning and the necessity of providing them with concrete experiences and opportunities to discover things for themselves (Davis, 1991). This is in contrast to a more traditional teaching approach in which children are seen as being passive recipients of information. The Piagetian constructivist theory is limited, however, in that although it recognises the importance of social and cultural factors these are secondary to the idea of developmental stages.

> In Piagetian theory, learning is predominantly individually centred, and development leads learning. Stages of development are both sequential and hierarchical and children cannot progress from one to another until a state of consolidation and readiness has been achieved. (Wood & Bennett, 1999)

Boulton-Lewis (1995) pointed out the dangers of teachers waiting until a child had reached the appropriate stage before introducing certain concepts, giving support to this idea of 'readiness' described above. In accepting Piagetian theory the role of the teacher is very much that of a facilitator and supporter.

Another important player in teachers' knowledge of how children learn and understand is Vygotsky whose theories have given rise to a social-constructivist framework. Children's learning and understanding are seen to be more dependent on experience than on developmental stages. Changes in a child's understanding come about, according to Vygotsky, through moving from an initial level of understanding which is rather vague to a level where the learner attempts to make sense of new knowledge, connecting it with prior knowledge. Those with greater knowledge and understanding have a key role to play in guiding the child from one level of understanding to another through what Vygotsky called the Zone of Proximal Development (ZPD). The influence of social-constructivist theory has led to a greater emphasis on teacher support through modelling and scaffolding (Lewis & Wray, 1995; the National Literacy Strategy, 1998; Waterland, 1985).

The importance of play in developing the young child's understanding has also been well documented (e.g. David, 1999) and is very much part of what early years practitioners know about child development. Whitebread (2000: 151–154) discusses Bruner's argument that play is essential to the development of children's intellectual ability.

> Play, in Bruner's view, is all about developing flexibility of thought. It provides opportunities to try out possibilities, to put different elements of a situation together in various ways, to look at problems from different viewpoints. (Whitebread, 2000: 152)

Teachers' knowledge of children's understanding has been influenced by the dominant theories described. From this knowledge notions of good early years' practice have arisen. The Early Years Curriculum Group (1998) took from research evidence the key factors in effective early years education. These included the importance of rooting children's early education in their prior knowledge and experience, the need for active and social involvement, the importance of partnership between teacher and learner and the necessary opportunities being provided for children to take responsibility for their actions (Early Years Curriculum Group, 1998: 2).

In terms of pedagogy these points were translated into opportunities that had to be provided in an early years' curriculum if children were to understand and learn. These were:

- active learning
- interactive learning
- decision making
- reflecting
- representing

(Early Years Curriculum Group, 1998: 2)

Does the *Curriculum Guidance for the Foundation Stage* (QCA, 2000) set out to meet these requirements? Certainly it acknowledges the importance of:

> Knowledge and understanding of the world: with opportunities for all children to solve problems, make decisions, experiment, predict, plan and question in a variety of contexts, and to explore and find out about their environment and people and places that have significance in their lives. (QCA, 2000: 9)

How the guidance sets about the task of translating these requirements into curricular guidance will be considered in the next section.

Curriculum Guidance for the Foundation Stage: A General Overview

First of all it would be appropriate to look in general terms at the organisation and the content of the guidance before going on to analyse some of the suggested practical recommendations, using the points identified by the Early Years

Curriculum Group (see previous section) as a framework. The guidance is divided into four sections, the two main sections address first of all the principles and supporting practice for effective early years education and then the areas of learning and early learning goals. Within the principles outlined can be found elements that relate to learning theory previously discussed in terms of children's understanding. Examples of these include:

> Early years experience should build on what children already know and can do and … an early years curriculum should (include) provision for the different starting points from which children develop their learning, building on what they can already do (and) relevant and appropriate content that matches the different levels of young children's needs. (QCA. 2000: 11)

Having outlined the principles for effective practice in early years settings the document provides supporting descriptions of what these principles mean and practical examples of how the principles can be turned into good practice. One example describes how, building on a child's experience of being in hospital, a teacher of a pre-school group of children set up a 'hospital' and in consultation with the children decided that the hospital needed a reception area with a telephone, an appointment book, pencils and a notepad. The children took on the roles of receptionist, doctors and nurses. In their different roles they began to 'write', scribbling and making approximations of letters and numbers (QCA 2000: 15). In this way the children's writing would develop but important social skills would also be fostered.

In this same section (QCA 2000: 20–24) effective learning and teaching are described and clearly explained.

> Learning for young children is a rewarding and enjoyable experience in which they explore, investigate, discover, create, practise, rehearse, repeat, revise and consolidate their developing knowledge, skills, understanding and attitudes. During the foundation stage, many of these aspects of learning are brought together effectively through playing and talking. (QCA 2000: 20)

> Teaching means systematically helping children to learn so that they are helped to make connections in their learning and are actively led forward, as well as helped to reflect on what they have already learned. (QCA 2000: 22)

Again this section gives clear practical examples of how the theory can be translated into good practice, each example easily recognised by early years practitioners as ways in which children can be assisted in their understanding.

The other main section addresses the areas of learning and early learning goals. The guidance is providing a curriculum that supports the attainment of *Early Learning Goals* (QCA, 1999). These goals are organised into six areas of learning that are almost identical to the earlier *Desirable Outcomes for Children's Learning* (SCAA, 1996). The areas are: personal, social and emotional development; communication, language and literacy; mathematical development; knowledge and understanding of the world: physical development and creative development. The supporting curriculum guidance is quick to point out that the areas are defined in order to assist practitioners with the planning of experiences and activities and not to suggest that children's understanding can be divided into discrete areas. Edwards and Knight (1994) discuss the concern of early years practitioners that a Key Stage 2 subject based curriculum is being inflicted on children at Key Stage 1 and even at pre-school stage, forcing teachers to introduce a traditional curriculum too early. Interestingly, Edwards and Knight do not dismiss out of hand the use of subjects for teachers' thinking about the curriculum.

> At some point, beginning practitioners will need to arrive at understandings of the structure of the material of the early years curriculum. We suggest that this is best done through analyses of the nature of subjects. Subjects are an accepted way of describing the knowledge that is important within our culture. (Edwards & Knight, 1994: 53)

They argue that the problem does not lie with the subjects themselves but with the traditional teaching of the subjects. It is important that the subjects are not taught in an abstract way but at the same time the framework of subjects can help 'both practitioners and learners to identify and use the discourses and understandings that they contain' (Edwards & Knight 1994: 53). This is very much in keeping with the stated position of the foundation stage curriculum guidance.

The guidance takes each area and identifies 'stepping stones' of progress towards the early learning goals. The knowledge, skills, understanding and attitudes are described that children will need to achieve the goals. The stepping stones are supported by practical examples of what children may typically do at the various stages and what the practitioner needs to do. Again, QCA make quite explicit the fact that although the stepping stones are presented in an hierarchical order it should not be expected that all children will conform to the sequence. Very much in keeping with a social-constructivist theory of children's understanding, building on children's prior knowledge is seen as being very important.

> As children move from one stepping stone to another, they take with them what they have already learned and continue to practise, refine and use their previous learning, so that learning becomes consolidated. (QCA, 2000: 27)

For example, in the section on Knowledge and understanding of the world, a child's description of a family wedding is followed up with the suggestion that this would be a good opportunity to explain the significance of special events, a stepping stone on the way to the early learning goal of children beginning to *know about their own cultures and beliefs and those of other people.*

The value of play and active learning is very much acknowledged by the QCA's guidance. Mathematical understanding, for example, is seen as being developed through stories, songs, games and imaginative play (QCA, 2000: 68) and, again, the practitioner is given many examples of practical activities to help the children on their way to attaining the early learning goals.

Relating the Guidance to Essential Elements Identified by the Early Years Curriculum Group (1998)

Having looked generally at the organisation of the *Curriculum Guidance for the Foundation Stage* (QCA, 2000) and the way in which it reflects what we know about teaching for understanding, it would be useful at this stage to return to the essential points identified by the Early Years Curriculum Group as being important to the development of a child's learning and understanding. The essential elements identified were *active learning, interactive learning, decision making, reflecting and representing.* (Early Years Curriculum Group, 1998). These elements were used as a framework by the group to consider the National Curriculum (DES, 1989) in terms of how it reflected research evidence on learning and understanding in the early years. The same framework will be used to analyse the new curriculum guidance, albeit in much less detail.

Active learning is advocated in the curriculum guidance through the many examples of recommended practical activities, e.g.

> Provide and encourage children to play with and talk about collections of objects that have similar and different properties, for example natural and made, size, colour, shape, texture, function. (QCA, 2000: 89 from *Knowledge and Understanding of the World*)

Interactive learning is described by the Early Years Curriculum Group as being either interaction with the teacher or with other children. The importance of scaffolding is stressed in child–teacher interaction. The area of *Communication, language and literacy* provides us with examples of scaffolding e.g.

> Respond to children and reply in words that extend and model the child's communication. (QCA, 2000: 49).

and also with examples of how to encourage pupil–pupil interaction:

> Encourage conversation and help children to respond to the contributions of others in role play and other activities. (QCA, 2000: 49).

Decision making is another requirement identified by the curriculum group from research that is seen as being essential if children are to make sense of their learning. From the area of *Physical development* it is recommended that teachers:

> Talk with children about their actions and encourage them to explore different ways of representing ideas and actions as they move. (QCA, 2000: 105).

From *Knowledge and Understanding of the World* teachers are asked to:

> Give opportunities to design practical, attractive environments, for example taking care of the flowerbeds or organising equipment outdoors. (QCA, 2000: 97)

Reflecting is about activating prior knowledge and building upon that knowledge. An example from the *Curriculum Guidance for the Foundation Stage* can be found in the area of Mathematical development

> Discuss with children how problems relate to others they have met and their different solutions. (QCA, 2000: 77)

Finally, the Early Years Curriculum Group (1998) identified *Representing* as a vital part of learning and understanding. By representing what they have learned in either spoken, physical or graphic form young children's understanding is formulated and reformulated. From the area of *Personal, social and emotional development* we find:

> Encourage children to explore and talk about new learning, valuing their ideas and ways of doing things. (QCA, 2000: 33)

From the area of *Creative development* teachers are asked to

> Provide children with opportunities to use their skills and explore concepts and ideas through their representations. (QCA, 2000: 121)

Conclusion

Early Learning Goals (QCA, 1999) replaced the earlier *Desirable Outcomes for Children's Learning* (SCAA, 1996) as a document that sets out what children should attain before embarking on the National Curriculum. Unlike its predecessor, however, the new document has the support of curriculum guidance that aims to help young children meet the learning goals in ways that match what research evidence has told us about children's learning and understanding. Children need to develop understanding in order to make connections with what they already know, to solve problems, to be creative, to reason, to make sense of what they are learning and, because of this, remember what they have learned and apply that learning in new contexts. The earlier document (SCAA, 1996), containing as it did only the final targets, could quite easily have led to practitioners delivering a totally inappropriate curriculum. This has been remedied by the publication of *Curriculum Guidance for the Foundation Stage* (QCA, 2000). Concern had been expressed (see Introduction) about the inappropriateness of what was being seen as the National Curriculum simply being diluted for pre-school children as they were rushed towards targets and baseline assessment. The new curriculum guidance should help to remedy this. Certainly, the curriculum addresses the needs and opportunities identified by the Early Years Curriculum Group as being essential for understanding and effective learning. Early years practitioners have been given permission, if they needed it, to plan a curriculum on what is known about developing children's understanding and learning. As a bonus, the whole of the Reception Year is included in the foundation stage and these children also now have a curriculum more suited to meeting their needs.

Correspondence

Any correspondence should be directed to Ms Eve English, University of Durham, School of Education, Leazes Road, Durham DH1 1TA, UK (eve.english@durham.ac.uk).

References

Boulton-Lewis, G. (1995) Memory, cognition, learning and teaching. In G. Boulton-Lewis and D. Catherwood. *The Early Years* (pp. 59–102). London: Pitman.

David, T. (1999) Changing minds: Young children learning. In T. David (ed.) *Young Children Learning* (pp. 1–12). London: Paul Chapman.

Davis, A. (1991) Piaget, teachers and education: Into the 1990s. In P. Light, S. Sheldon and M. Woodhead (eds) *Learning to Think* (pp. 16–31). London: Routledge.

Department for Education and Science (DES) (1989) *The National Curriculum*. London: HMSO.

Early Years Curriculum Group (1998) *Interpreting the National Curriculum at Key Stage 1*. Buckingham: Open University Press.

Edwards, A. and Knight, P. (1994) *Effective Early Years Education*. Buckingham: Open University Press.

Lewis, M. and Wray, D. (1995) *Developing Children's Non-fiction Writing: Working with Writing Frames*. Leamington Spa: Scholastic.

Newton, D (2000) What do we mean by teaching for understanding? In L. Newton (ed.) *Meeting the Standards in Primary Science* (pp. 191–203). London: Routledge Falmer.

Qualifications and Curriculum Authority (2000) *Curriculum Guidance for the Foundation Stage*. London: Department for Education and Employment.

School Curriculum and Assessment Authority (1996) *Nursery Education, Desirable Outcomes for Children's Learning*. London: Department for Education and Employment.

Waterland, E. (1985) *Read With Me – An Apprenticeship Approach to Reading*. Stroud: Thimble Press.

Whitebread, D. (2000) Teaching children to think, reason, solve problems and be creative. In D. Whitebread (ed.) *The Psychology of Teaching and Learning in the Primary School* (pp. 140–164). London: Routledge Falmer.

Wood, E. and Bennett, N. (1999) Progression and continuity in early childhood education: Tensions and contradictions. *International Journal of Early Years Education* 7 (1).

Notes on Contributors

Dr Sue Beverton

Sue Beverton taught in schools for 16 years before moving into higher education. She spent many years delivering in-service work before her current post, being Primary English Convenor for initial teacher training programmes at the School of Education, University of Durham. She is also Course Leader of the BA (Ed) with QTS. Her research interests include the evolving nature of English as a school subject and the effects upon pupils' learning of English of the transfer from primary to secondary school.

Dr Tony Blake

After a number of years in primary school as a classroom teacher and deputy headteacher, Tony Blake joined the staff of the Department of Education in the University of Newcastle upon Tyne in 2000. He is the tutor in charge of the primary science programmes and has a particular interest in geology and the history of science.

Dr Andrew Davis

Andrew Davis publishes in the field of educational policy and mathematics education from the perspective of analytical philosophy in which he originally trained. He taught in primary schools for many years and is currently Senior Lecturer in Education at Durham University, directing the primary mathematics provision as well as being Course Leader for the Primary PGCE programme. His publications include *Developing Understanding in Primary Mathematics* (1994, with Diedre Petit, published by Falmer Press), *The Limits of Educational Assessment* (1998, Blackwell) and *Educational Assessment: A Critique of Current Policy* (1999, Impact Series No. 1: Philosophy of Education Society of Great Britain).

Ms Eve English

Eve English is a lecturer on the Initial Teacher Training course at the School of Education, University of Durham. She teaches English and also supports students' school experience as a tutor. She is particularly interested in the Induction Year for Newly Qualified Teachers. Prior to joining the university she was headteacher of an infant school.

Mr John Halocha

Following a successful career in primary education, John Halocha moved into initial teacher training, initially at Westminster College, Oxford, and then at the University of Durham, where he was tutor in charge of primary geography. In 2000 he moved to a Senior Lectureship in education at Bishop Grosseteste University College, Lincoln. He also has a interest in ICT in education.

Mr Steve Higgins

After teaching in primary schools, Steve Higgins joined the staff at the Department of Education at Newcastle University. He is now a senior lecturer and teaches on the mathematics on the primary PGCE course. His research interests are in teaching thinking, mathematics and ICT. He was project manager for the TTA-funded study of *Effective Pedagogy Using ICT for Literacy and Numeracy in Primary Schools*.

Dr Peter Millward

Peter Millward works at the University of Durham, where his wide range of expertise, both as a primary teacher and lecturer, involves him in a range of courses. In the past he has worked in primary initial teacher training, particularly in the area of English and drama. More recently he has been significantly involved in the innovative Childhood and the Arts course based at the University's Stockton Campus.

Professor Douglas Newton

Doug Newton is in the Department of Education, Newcastle University, where he lectures on science and technology education and teaching for understanding. He is particularly interested in the nature of understanding, the mental processes of understanding, and how to support understanding in the classroom. His recent book, *Teaching for Understanding* (Routledge/Falmer) examines these in some detail and offers practical advice on how to foster understanding in a variety of disciplines and with a variety of learners.

Dr Lynn Newton

After working for many years in primary schools, Lynn became an advisory teacher for primary science and technology. She then moved to the University of Newcastle upon Tyne, where she was responsible for primary science as well as being Director of the PGCE programme for seven years. She moved to Durham University in 1997, initially to be Course Leader for the BSc (Ed) degree for primary science and ICT specialists. She is now Director of Primary Programmes and Primary Science convenor for initial training and in-service programmes. Her most recent books are *Co-ordinating Science Across the Primary School* (Falmer Press, 1998) and *Meeting the Standards in Primary Science* (Routledge Falmer, 2000).

Dr Anthony Parton

Anthony Parton joined the staff of the University of Durham School of Education in 1999 after a varied career in the world of the Arts. His expertise is very much in the area of creative expression and childhood and the Arts and he is one of the lead tutors on the Childhood and the Arts programme at the University's Stockton Campus, working closely with Peter Millward.